D0239455

# RISEN FROM THE DEAD

Colaiste Oideachais Mhuire Gan Smal
Luimneach
MIC LIBRARY
WITHDRAWN FROM STOCK

*

HENRY WANSBROUGH O.S.B.

# RISEN
# FROM THE
# DEAD

 St Paul Publications

MM37

## ACKNOWLEDGEMENT

The Bible quotations in this publication are from the Jerusalem Bible published and © 1966, 1967 and 1968 by Darton Longman & Todd Ltd. and Doubleday & Co. Inc. and are used by permission of the publishers.

Coláiste
Mhuire Gan Smal
Luimneach
Class No. 236·8 LAW
Acc. No. 51,610

**St Paul Publications**
Middlegreen, Slough SL3 6BT

© St Paul Publications 1978
Nihil obstat: D.A. Valente ssp
Imprimatur: F. Diamond vg, Northampton
First published in 1978
Printed in Great Britain by the Society of St Paul
085439 150 9

# CONTENTS

I. — PAUL ... ... ... ... ... ... ...     9

  1. Before Paul ... ... ... ... ... ...   10
    a) A Hymn ... ... ... ... ... ...   10
    b) A Fragment of Tradition ... ... ...   12
    c) Biblical Theology ... ... ... ...   15
  2. The Source of Paul's Gospel ... ... ...   17
  3. The Early Letters ... ... ... ... ...   19
  4. The Great Epistles ... ... ... ... ...   23
    a) The Body of Christ ... ... ... ...   23
    b) The Nature of the Risen Body ... ...   26
    c) The New Spirit ... ... ... ... ...   29
    d) Conclusion ... ... ... ... ... ...   30
  5. The Captivity Epistles ... ... ... ...   31
    a) Authorship ... ... ... ... ... ...   31
    b) Paul's Opponents ... ... ... ...   32
    c) The Resurrection ... ... ... ... ...   33
  6. Conclusion ... ... ... ... ... ... ...   39
  Interlude: 1. Historicity and the Gospels ...   40
          2. An Example: "On the third day"   42

II. — THE SYNOPTIC GOSPELS ... ...   45

  1. The Order of Composition ... ... ...   45
  2. Mark ... ... ... ... ... ... ... ...   48
  3. Matthew ... ... ... ... ... ... ...   53
    a) The Empty Tomb ... ... ... ...   53
    b) The Final Commission ... ... ...   57

4. Luke ... ... ... ... ... ... ... ...    59
   a) The Empty Tomb   ... ... ... ...   59
   b) The Road to Emmaus   ... ... ...   63
   c) Appearance at Jerusalem   ... ... ...   66
   d) The Final Blessing   ... ... ... ...   70
5. Conclusion ... ... ... ... ... ... ...   71

III. — THE GOSPEL OF JOHN   ... ...   75

Preliminary   ... ... ... ... ... ... ...   75
1. Resurrection Stories ... ... ... ... ...   76
   a) The Empty Tomb   ... ... ... ...   76
   b) The Appearances in the Upper Room   81
   c) Meeting at the Lake (Epilogue)   ...   84
   d) Conclusions ... ... ... ... ... ...   88
2. The Risen Christ in His Ministry   ... ...   90
   a) The Resurrection is Already   ... ...   90
   b) The Promise of the Spirit ... ... ...   92

IV. — WHAT ACTUALLY HAPPENED? ...   97

   a) The Bultmann School   ... ... ...   97
   b) And the Bones of Jesus?   ... ... ...   102
   c) Conclusions ... ... ... ... ... ...   104

# PLAN

The purpose is chronological, but the form a sandwich. The purpose was to follow out the doctrine of the resurrection as it develops in the New Testament in the principal writings (excluding the non-Pauline letters). In fact this has worked out so that the beginning and end of this investigation turn out to be a primarily theological investigation of Paul's and John's presentation of the resurrection, while the intervening part has been a more historical enquiry into the gospel resurrection narratives. In the course of writing I was so frequently asked in a jocular fashion, 'Well, did it happen?' that a short section has been added at the end which pulls together some threads in current controversies.

# I.

# PAUL

A biblical consideration of the doctrine of the resurrection of Jesus can most suitably begin from the teaching found in Paul. Unreflectively the Christian is drawn to start from a consideration of the gospel narratives, and especially from the story of the empty tomb. But chronologically this is entirely unjustified, for the earliest of the gospels as documents is easily a decade later than the last of Paul's letters. And in fact, no matter how primitive the tradition on which they rely (and this will have to be examined later in its due place), the actual narratives of the gospel show a developed form of tradition which has been enriched by prolonged reflection and meditation. Even Paul's teaching itself is not the first starting-point; buried within these letters are fragments of tradition which go back behind Paul. The pattern of our study, then, must be first the primitive tradition before Paul; next Paul's view of the resurrection; then the historical and theological material contained in the synoptic gospels; and finally the completion of the New Testament teaching in the gospel of John.

# 1 — BEFORE PAUL

## a) *A Hymn*

Of the primitive teaching before Paul there are three entirely separate and different fragments which deserve special consideration, a hymn, a credal statement and a piece of theology. All these are found in Paul's letters, embedded there, and comparatively easily recognisable as separable from Paul's own writing.

The first of these passages shows that the idea of resurrection should not be seen in isolation. There were other ways of expressing Christ's position which were also current in the early Christian community. In his letter to the Philippians Paul is exhorting his beloved community to generosity and humility, when he suddenly breaks into an extended statement about the generosity and humility of Christ. On linguistic grounds as well as its disproportion to the context it appears that Paul is reminding them of a hymn which is already familiar to them from the liturgy. Paul himself added a phrase here and there to the hymn, but the original of the last stanza has been convincingly reconstructed by J. Jeremias:

> Therefore God raised him high
> and gave him the name which is above all other names
> so that all beings should bend the knee at the name of Jesus
> and every tongue acclaim Jesus Christ as Lord.
>
> (Phil 2.9-11)

The crucial point about this quotation is that the central point for the hymn is not the resurrection itself but the exaltation of Jesus. The Greek word used for 'raised high' is from a quite different stem from that used by Paul for the resurrection. There are a number of other passages in the New Testament where the idea of exaltation occurs without any clear reference to a resurrection in the sense of a raising from the tomb or from the dead. The gospel of John uses this terminology almost habitually, often with more direct reference to the raising of Jesus onto the cross than to his raising from the dead (e.g., Jn 12.32-33). In the early speeches of the Acts of the Apostles — it is irrelevant to the present point whether they represent a primitive theology or not, for we are trying to show only that the ideas of exaltation and resurrection occur independently — Peter speaks frequently of the exaltation of Jesus as an idea distinct from, though related to, that of resurrection (Acts 3.13; 5.31). The same is true of other New Testament writers (1 Peter 3.21; Heb 1.13, etc.). C.F. Evans argues: [1] "It is thus possible that the concept of exaltation to the right hand of God and of the consequent share in God's authority and rule was prior to the idea of resurrection in establishing belief in Jesus' lordship and messiahship, for it leads directly to it, while resurrection from the dead, as such, does not". The relative priority of the ideas is not at stake, and this would be difficult to establish firmly, but only the independence of the concepts.

Nor are these the only ways in which Christ's position is described. The position of Christ as the authoritative leader of Christians, their guide and hope and model and Lord, is complex, and the New Testament writers grope their way to find different expressions for it. Different writers express it in different ways, and often the same writer in different ways, struggling to express different aspects. Thus in Paul's earliest letters the dominant idea is that Jesus will come from heaven to lead Christians in his triumphal procession (1 Thess 4.16). In Matthew we find side by side, providing two originally independent and self-sufficient statements of belief, the

---

[1] *Resurrection and the New Testament*, (SCM Press, 1970), p. 137

11

story of the empty tomb and the saying in which the gospel reaches its climax: "All authority in heaven and on earth has been given to me" (Mt 28.18). In John's gospel the authority of Christ is most vividly translated into terms of a saving transformation which has already occurred through Christ and in which Christ is present and active through his Spirit. According to Willi Marxsen [2] these could all be expressed in yet another formulation: "the cause of Jesus continues; or in the words of the hymn 'Still he comes today' ". In fact these are no more than two further aspects, or translations into other language of myth and poetry, of the basic truth which the New Testament formulas are trying to express.

It is, therefore, important to realise that the resurrection language which eventually triumphed almost to the exclusion of all other modes of expression, and certainly to the extent of becoming the predominant symbol of Christ's position, was originally only one among many languages. In at least one of the traditions before Paul, expressed in the hymn of Philippians, it was not the dominant idea. Whether it was the influence of Paul in the early Church, or of another theologian, which made the theme of resurrection *the* symbol of Christ's triumph would be the subject of a fascinating study for which there is no place here. Was it perhaps because of the visual and imaginative appeal of this mode of expression? In any case, this mode did not originally stand alone.

### b) *A Fragment of Tradition*

The second pre-Pauline fragment preserved in Paul's letters which is to be examined is a credal statement

---

[2] *The Resurrection of Jesus of Nazareth,* (Eng. tr. SCM Press, 1970), p. 141

at the beginning of 1 Corinthians 15. Paul quotes this passage as a piece of tradition which he received and passed on to his converts at Corinth. There is another instance in 1 Corinthians of just such a block of traditional material, where Paul also uses the same technical terms for receiving and passing on tradition. To the Jews, of course, with their reverence for traditional teaching, and especially in view of the importance of substantiating any religious interpretation by appeal to previous religious teachers, the process of learning by heart was a central part of receiving instruction. There are prodigious statistics of the amount of learning by heart which was involved in education and of feats of memory demanded of and performed by pupils.[3] Thus it was only to be expected that part of instruction in the Christian message should consist in learning some basic facts by heart. The other block of such material in 1 Corinthians concerns the institution of the eucharist (11.23ff). This also can be isolated from the Pauline surround on linguistic and other grounds,[4] so that one can be pretty sure of the extent of this pre-Pauline fragment of tradition. In the case of the resurrection-appearances tradition it is impossible to obtain such an entirely satisfactory result, for Paul includes his own experience, which he obviously did not receive from the tradition, and this poses the problem of when the traditional material ends and Paul's addition begins.

Well then, in the first place, I taught you what I had been taught myself, namely:
> that Christ died for our sins in accordance with the scriptures,
> that he was buried, and

---

[3] Birger Gerhardsson, *Memory and Manuscript* (Gleerup, Lund, 1964), pp. 122-170
[4] See J. Jeremias, *The Eucharistic Words of Jesus* (SCM Press, 1964), pp. 101-105

that he was raised to life on the third day in accordance
with the scriptures;

that he appeared first to Cephas
and then to the twelve;
next he appeared to more than five hundred of the
brothers at the same time, most of whom are still
alive though some have died;

next he appeared to James
then to all the apostles
and last of all he appeared to me; it was as though
I was born when no one expected it.

(1 Cor 15.3-8)

There is any number of literary and exegetical problems about this passage. What is the exact pattern? There
are clearly three triplets, in each of which the last
member is lengthened, but are the second and third
triplets really parallel to the first? Is there any significance in the balance of the conjunctions "next", "then",
etc? A more important problem is connected with the
meaning of the word translated "he appeared". The word
used (*ophthe*) is not entirely straightforward, and, it is
claimed, does not obviously refer merely to simple seeing. Faced with this primitive report of factual appearances, a number of scholars who wish to water down
the reality of the bodily resurrection of Jesus have
claimed, with more or less strength, that this *ophthe*
represents something approximating more to an internal,
psychological experience than to physical sight. The
most authoritative German dictionary of the New Testament, after a long investigation of the usage of the
term, concludes that "it does not mean in the first
instance that they saw Him, with an emphasis on seeing,
e.g., in contrast to hearing. It means rather He encoun-
tered them as the risen, living Lord; they experienced

His presence".[5] Although there certainly are instances in which "seeing God" is used in a transferred or poetical sense of a non-visual experience of God, here there is no question of seeing God, or even an angel. It is a question of seeing the risen Christ, and though the element of awe which accompanies an experience of the divine is no doubt intended as well, there are no real grounds — other than inherent prejudice on the part of scholars — for denying that the straightforward sense of visual sight is intended.

Now Paul wrote his letter to the Corinthians in the early or middle 50's of the first century. But he evangelised the Corinthians at the beginning of the 50's, and it is at that time (as he claims) that this piece was already traditional material, hardly more than a dozen years after the resurrection itself. By that time, then, there was already standard in the Christian communities a list of factual evidence to the resurrection-appearances (the second triplet) and a theological analysis, heavy with scriptural reference, of what had happened (the first triplet). It is surely on this factual basis that all later discussion must build.

c) *Biblical Theology*

A third piece of pre-Pauline tradition still to be mentioned is more in the nature of one sample among many. We have just seen that in the most primitive traditional statement of the resurrection the occurrence is stressed as being "in accordance with the scriptures". From the very beginning of the Church when Christians, or indeed Jesus himself, tried to explain the events and significance of Jesus' life it was in terms of the fulfil-

---

[5] W. Michaelis in *Theological Dictionary of the New Testament*, ed. G. Friedrich, vol. V (Eerdmans, Grand Rapids, 1967), p. 358. The article begins on p. 315

ment of the Old Testament. This appears most clearly in the speech of Peter at Pentecost in the Acts of the Apostles, which attempts to explain what has happened in terms of three texts of scripture. But again and again in the New Testament the argument is used that the texts of scripture are literally fulfilled only in Jesus; this was clearly the method of the earliest theological reflection. One of the texts whose use is both most widespread and most primitive in the tradition is Psalm 110.1:

> "The Lord said to my Lord
> Sit at my right hand
> Until I make your enemies a footstool for you".

In the gospels this text is used in controversy with the Pharisees to show Jesus beating the Jewish scripture scholars at their own game.[6] But it was already used far earlier to explain the resurrection. The primitive character of this usage is shown not primarily by its occurrence in Peter's speech at Pentecost, for the date of composition of that speech as we now have it is vigorously controverted, but by the way Paul simply alludes to it as something totally familiar. In Romans 8.34 he says "and there at God's right hand he stands and pleads for us", or in 1 Corinthians 15.25 "for he must be king until he has put all his enemies under his feet". In the later epistles also he uses the same allusion: "you must look for the things that are in heaven, where Christ is, sitting at God's right hand" (Col 3.1, cf. Eph 1.20). This unexplained and allusive nature of Paul's reference to the text of the psalm, and also its spread through widely differing authors of

---

[6] That this is the chief point of the passage may be seen from its inclusion by Mark among three other controversies with the Jewish authorities (Mk 12.13-37), cf B. Lindars, *New Testament Apologetic* (SCM, 1961), pp. 46-47

the New Testament, not only Paul and Mark, but also Hebrews and 1 Peter, suggest that it was a way of explaining the resurrection which goes back even beyond Paul.

## 2 — THE SOURCE OF PAUL'S GOSPEL

To isolate and analyse the importance of the resurrection in Paul is an almost impossible task, for it embraces his whole view. His whole preaching is centred on Christ, and his whole view of Christ is determined by the resurrection. "Resurrection implies Christ's lordship, his return, the *judgement* and the *salvation of those who believe* . . . What the 'gospel of Christ' or 'gospel of God' which Paul preached was: that Christ had died and that God had raised him, that Christ is Lord, that the Lord will return, that the *apistoi* will be destroyed, that the believers would be saved".[7] Here it will be possible to do no more than pick up the immediate resonances of the resurrection in a severely limited part of its range.

In so far as it is possible to discern the sources of Paul's specifically Christian thinking, and in particular his view of Christ, they appear to be twofold. He puts forward as the basic experience of his vocation and apostolate the independent revelation of Christ described in the Acts of the Apostles on the road to Damascus, an experience of Christ as Lord. Some hesitations about the historicity of the details of this incident as described in Acts cannot be avoided, for in Acts Luke frequently expresses his theology by means of such graphic and easily imagined scenes (e.g., the coming of the Spirit at Pentecost); the same is true of

---

[7] E.P. Sanders, *Paul and Palestinian Judaism* (SCM, 1977), pp. 446-7

B

the infancy narratives of his gospel. In this particular incident, the narrative is formally modelled upon vocation narratives of the Old Testament, and contains clear allusions to Old Testament appearances (e.g., Daniel 10.7-8), by which the meaning of the scene may be perceived.[8] But, whatever conventions Luke used in his composition of this story, the force and value of his work is seen in the extent to which it corresponds to Paul's own view of Christ as expounded in his letters.

The other source of Paul's Christian theology was, of course, the Christian community, and, as we have seen, both the liturgical hymn quoted in Philippians 2.6-11 and the theology represented by Paul's casual use of Psalm 110 point to the same concentration on the lordship of Christ. Another tiny indication is worth citing because of its primitive character: Paul quotes the liturgical cry *marana tha* (Our Lord, come), whose retention in Aramaic shows its primitive origin.[9] There may well be also a reference to the Christian confession of Christ as Lord concealed in 1 Corinthians 12.3. This suggests that Christians were invited to proclaim the frequent formula of loyalty to the emperor "Caesar is Lord", coupled with and reinforced by its opposite, "Jesus is cursed" precisely because their usual formula was "Jesus is Lord" which was felt to detract from the loyalty due to the Roman emperor — as indeed it did. In all but this last reference the lordship of Christ is connected with his resurrection, and would lead on to Paul's own expression of this matter.

---

[8] Cf. G. Lohfink, *Paulus vor Damaskus* (Katholisches Bibelwerk, Stuttgart, 1965); E. Haenchen, *Die Apostelgeschichte* (Vandenhoeck u. Ruprecht, Göttingen, 1965), pp. 268-277

[9] 1 Cor 16.22. The words in the Greek text can be divided differently, *maran atha,* so that it becomes a confession ("The Lord comes") rather than a prayer, but the division proposed in the text is more likely.

# 3 — THE EARLY LETTERS

Central as the conception of the risen Christ as Lord remains throughout Paul's writing, it is not fully explained until the last part of his writing career, when he was forced to spell it out in the Captivity Epistles in reply to challenges from opponents. Paul is no academic theologian composing treatises in logical order, but is a pastoral writer, responding to problems and answering questions which arise in the communities he founded. Of course at different times there are, over and above the challenges he receives from the individual communities, preoccupations of his own which spring more or less readily to the fore; but these, too, arise often from the stimuli of questions from his communities, and tend to vary as time goes on. Consonant with his preoccupation primarily with the needs of his communities is Paul's concentration on soteriology; his primary concern is with the salvation of men and how they are brought totally into the sphere of God. Until the position of Christ is challenged at the end, Paul takes it for granted and concentrates on man. His gospel is, after all, the good news for men, not an abstract discussion of theology, and as such deals primarily with how the Christ-event affects men. In any case — and no doubt his response to stimuli and the development of his own thoughts are closely interrelated — Paul's thoughts on the risen Christ can most conveniently be considered at three successive periods, the first represented by the letters to the Thessalonians, but carrying over into First Corinthians, the second by the Great Epistles and the third primarily by the Captivity Epistles, Colossians and Ephesians.

In the first of these three periods Paul's thinking, and so his view of the risen Christ, is dominated by eschatological expectation. The Messiah was to come, according to Jewish hopes, to found God's final kingdom, to bring to realisation the kingship of God on earth and to make all things new. In detail the hopes varied according to individual temperament or affiliation to different groups. Some would put the emphasis on peace, healing, plenty and satisfied idleness, whereas others would stress more the obedience of all creation to God's will, or the annihilation of wickedness and its perpetrators, pointing the finger now at the oppressing Romans, now at unbelieving gentiles in general. But an integral part of this hope was that the establishment of God's kingdom would be the fulfilment and completion of all that was destined by God.

It was the main burden of Jesus' teaching and message that in him the kingship of God was reaching this completion, that harvest time had come and the fields were white for harvest. This was the significance of his bringing healing of sickness, forgiveness of sin and the gift of God's peace. His parables are full of challenge to decision because the moment of judgement has come and the time is short. So in the first teaching which we have after the resurrection it is not surprising to find a preoccupation with the final conclusion of all things. It was clear that in one sense everything had already been completed, and Christians seemed to have the sensation of sitting on their packed suitcases waiting for the taxi to arrive.

The problem for the Thessalonians to which Paul responds was that they were shocked by the death of some of their number; it is to reassure them about this that Paul writes his first letter. Paul, on his visit to Thessalonika during which he brought them the good news of Christ, may well have taught them that Christ had conquered death both for himself and for us in such a way that they could find the death of one of their number a seeming contradiction of the Christian message. Christ has brought the kingdom of God and in the kingdom of God there is no death. One could well imagine someone reading some of the statements in Paul's letters, that Christ has overcome death and the Christian is no more to die, in a literalist way and unaware of the subtleties of meaning in the word "death", and finding the actual death of a Christian a direct contradiction or even refutation of the whole Christian message. Paul has speedily to restore the balance by explaining what he means.

> We believe that Jesus died and rose again, and that it will be the same for those who have died in Jesus; God will bring them with him . . . Those who have died in Christ will be the first to rise, and then we who are still alive will be taken up, together with them, to meet the Lord in the air (1 Thess 4.14,16-17).

The imagery of this passage is that of a triumphal procession. Jesus will come with his triumphal retinue consisting of those who have already died in Christ, and those who are still alive will advance to meet him. The word used for this meeting (*apantesis*) conjures up a whole world of imagery in its hellenistic context, for it is used of the formal greeting made by the burghers of a town who go out to welcome a triumphal general or emperor on tour. The scene is one of homage and — often sycophantic — acknowledgement that the general or emperor comes to the city as a saviour. In the context of the imperial cult, as it then was in the Eastern Mediterranean, the approaching dignitary was often hailed in divine terms. The same ideas borrowed from the hellenistic cult of rulers form the context for the expressions about the *parousia* of Christ which are used frequently in the two letters to the Thessalonians but otherwise only once, in 1 Corinthians 15. This *parousia* is no ordinary coming, but is the solemn arrival in pomp and circumstance of a monarch to save or restore a city. One interesting overtone of this word is seen from the fact that in several cases a city begins to number its years from such a visit ("x years after the *parousia* of Y"), indicating that this visit formed the beginning of a new life or new era for the city; just so the *parousia* of Christ marks the end of one era and the beginning of a new world. This coming marks the final salvation, in hope of which the Thessalonians are encouraged to live their Christian lives:

> "may he so confirm your hearts in holiness that you may be blameless at the coming of our Lord Jesus Christ" (1 Thess 3.13).

> "may you all be kept safe for the coming of our Lord Jesus Christ" (5.23).

The hellenistic terminology used in these letters may have suggested that Paul is drawing also on hellenistic ideology. This is important, for Christ is represented in this complex of ideas as a God who is manifesting himself to save his people. It might then be claimed — and indeed frequently has been claimed [10] — that, when Christ is here put in the position normally held by a divinised emperor, no more is being attributed to him than the curious sort of divine status which was accorded in the Eastern Roman Empire to the emperor. The true background, however, is not the hellenistic cult of rulers but the Old Testament; Paul draws his ideas from the Old Testament and merely uses hellenistic language to convey them. For in the eschatological writing of the Old Testament and of contemporary Jewish literature it is always God who will come to establish finally the new age which is the completion of his plan. In the eschatological battle "Yahweh will

---

[10] Most recently in *The Myth of the Incarnate God,* ed. John Hick (SCM Press, 1977)

take the field . . . on that day his feet will rest on the Mount of Olives . . . Yahweh your God will come" (Zech 14.3-5), or at the final judgement "The Lord you are seeking will suddenly enter his temple" (Mal 3.1). This place of Yahweh in the expectation has now been taken by the Lord Jesus, and this is one of the strongest arguments to show that the title of Lord is meant in a strong sense which can only indicate the divinity.

The connection of all this with Christ's resurrection may have begun to seem rather distant, and so it is necessary to pull the threads together. The whole procession only occurs in imitation of the resurrection of Jesus, and it is a fair assumption that since Christians obtain their place in the triumph by virtue of their resurrection in imitation of Christ's, so Jesus too holds his place by virtue of his resurrection: "we believe that Jesus died and rose again, and that it will be the same for those who have died in Jesus".


## 4 — THE GREAT EPISTLES

### a) *The Body of Christ*

By the time Paul comes to write First Corinthians his thoughts on the resurrection have developed considerably, and this in two directions: the risen Christ is the first-fruits of a risen humanity, and also Paul can say something about the quality of what is risen.

The first of these points is connected with the doctrine of the body of Christ which is the Church. On several occasions in the letter Paul's teaching on practical matters is founded on his conviction that Christians form the body of Christ. It is wrong for a

23

Christian to join his body sexually to that of a prostitute because he is taking part of Christ's body and joining that to the body of a prostitute in such a realistic and total way that the two become one flesh (1 Cor 6.15-17). The union of all Christians in one body is also expressed by their sharing in the one eucharistic loaf which is the body of Christ (1 Cor 10.17). The exact logical connection between these two meanings of "body" is not clear; it would perhaps be more true to say that Paul himself does not distinguish at all between them, for in his next section he equates disunity in the eucharistic celebration, disregard there for other members of Christ, with failing to recognise the body of the Lord (1 Cor 11.17-27); it is impossible to tell in which sense he is using the word "body", and most probably he is using it in both senses at once. Finally he turns his attention to the body itself and its constitution: in Christ's body, just as in a human body, there are many parts, each with its own function and part to play, but it is one because we are all enlivened by the same Spirit.

What Paul means here, and in what sense he understands our sharing of life in the Spirit, becomes clear by comparison with his teaching in other letters. In Philippians he is considering the possibility of his death for Christ's sake, and the strength given him by the Spirit of Christ, when he goes on to say that "Life to me, of course, is Christ" (Phil 1.21). Or in Galatians 2.20 "It is no longer I who live, but Christ lives in me". This is in virtue of the life of the Spirit within the Christian. It is no longer the spirit of ordinary man which informs the Christian, but this has been superseded by the Spirit of Christ which now informs him. The important passage on baptism in Romans shows that by baptism — in which the Spirit of Christ is imparted to us — we take on Christ's history as our own. What happened to him is now what has happened

24

to us; so total is our union to him: "When we were baptised into Christ, it was into his death that we were baptised; in other words, when we were baptised we went into the tomb with him and joined him in death, so that as Christ was raised from the dead by the Father's glory, we too might live a new life" (Rom 6.3-4).

Since this is Paul's view of our union of life with Christ, our vital sharing with him, it is no surprise that we are to share also his resurrection: he is "the first-fruits of all who have fallen asleep . . . Just as all men die in Adam, so all men will be brought to life in Christ; but all of them in their proper order: Christ as the first-fruits and then, after the coming of Christ, those who belong to him" (1 Cor 15:21-23). There is the same gradual process and the same priority as we saw in the letter to the Thessalonians, but the simple imagery of the triumphal procession has gone, and been succeeded by a more profound notion of the sharing of nature with Christ through his Spirit. The Adam-symbolism developed in Romans 5 makes this still clearer: as Adam was the principle and progenitor of natural humanity, from whom life flowed to men, so Christ is the principle and progenitor of a new humanity, from whom life flows to members of his body.

The only puzzle which remains, in view of the vital link between Christ and Christians, is the partial dislocation between them. Christ is risen but Christians are not. Although we are already "in Christ Jesus" (Rom 8.1) and already "a new creation" (2 Cor 5.17), nevertheless, in these letters, our salvation is still in the future: "God, who raised the Lord from the dead, *will* by his power raise us up too" (1 Cor 6.14); "we *shall be* saved through him" (Rom 5.9); "if you believe in your heart that God raised him from the dead, then you *will be* saved" (Rom 10.9). Perhaps the most striking dislocation is in Romans 6.5, "If in union with

25

Christ we *have* imitated his death, we *shall* also imitate him in his resurrection". It would at first sight seem reasonable that if Christians are the body of Christ and if Christ is risen, Christians too should be risen. But to this Paul makes two replies. Firstly he grants that "our homeland is in heaven" (Phil 3.20); the term translated "homeland" is a political one, implying that our citizenship and citizen-rights are in heaven; it is there and not on earth that we should feel at home, that we have, so to speak, voting-rights and all the other privileges which a citizen has; and, by contrast, on earth we are now natural exiles, or fish out of water.

In the same passage Paul goes on to say that "from heaven comes the saviour we are waiting for, the Lord Jesus Christ, and he *will* transfigure these wretched bodies of ours into copies of his glorious body" (Phil 3.20-21). This is the second part of his answer: we are not yet transformed in the same way as Christ is, but this is to take place in our own resurrection. In 1 Corinthians 15 Paul makes valiant attempts to explain what precisely this transformation will be (35-53). The question is not easy, and nor is his answer.

b) *The Nature of the Risen Body*

First he is concerned to give what seems to be an example of analogy. He is concerned to show that there is both continuity and discontinuity between the earthly body and the heavenly body, and he gives the grain of wheat as an example because there is continuity and yet transformation. This is followed up by a volley of analogies, or perhaps of what may be called family-likeness concepts, where there is a good deal of similarity in the object classified under one head but not absolute identity; the examples are "flesh", "body" and "brightness":

26

Everything that is flesh is not the same flesh: there is human flesh, animals' flesh, the flesh of birds and the flesh of fish. Then there are heavenly bodies and there are earthly bodies; but the heavenly bodies have a beauty of their own and the earthly bodies a different one. The sun has its brightness, the moon a different brightness, and the stars a different brightness, and the stars differ from each other in brightness".

What Paul is trying to illustrate is how in the resurrection the body can be the same body but be different in quality. He then goes on to say just how it is transformed after the model of Christ's risen body. He uses four pairs of contrasting features, of which the fourth is more a summing up of the others than a new advance. In each of these pairs the central feature is a removal of limitation and a transfer into the divine sphere by sharing in a property which is recognised as a divine property.

"The thing that is sown is perishable, but what is raised is imperishable" grants to the risen body the divine attribute which goes with God's eternity, in explicit contrast to man's transience: "To you a thousand years are a single day, a yesterday now over, an hour of the night" (Ps 90.4) or, stressing the contrast, "My days are vanishing like smoke . . . whereas you, Yahweh, remain for ever" (Ps 102.3,12). So in becoming imperishable in the resurrection the body is transferred from the changeableness of human life into the eternity of the divine.

"The thing that is sown is weak but what is raised is strong" claims a divine attribute which had always been Israel's protection and hope. It was Yahweh's strong right arm which saved them from Egypt and gave them the Land. In the Old Testament power and strength are the direct evidence of the presence of the

Spirit, which descends in a rushing wind and gives power to God's chosen representatives to deliver his people from oppression. In the New Testament Christ's "powers" are the word used especially by Luke for his miracles as signs of God's presence at work in him, and the coming of the kingdom "in power" (Mk 9.1) is the consummation of the age when God finally takes over. By contrast "weakness" is a general word for everything human and fallible. So here too the risen body is to be released from the limitations of the present world to share in the divine.

Perhaps this transfer is shown most strongly of all by "the thing that is sown is contemptible, but what is raised is glorious". God's glory is an awesome concept, something which comes as close as possible to the divinity itself. Man cannot look on God's glory and live, and in the stupendous vision at the vocation of Ezekiel all he is allowed to see is "something that *looked like* the glory of Yahweh" (Ezek 1.28). Even after contact with God, the glory with which Moses' face glowed was such that the Israelites could not look on it (2 Cor 3.7). In the temple the symbol of God's glory is the sign of his presence, which is an active presence, the assurance of his protection and strength over Israel. It is in particular, of course, an eschatological concept, for at the end, when they have been purified, all nations will come to behold the glory of God (Is 60.3; Hab 2.14); and at the eschatological visitation in the gospels Christ will come in the glory of his Father (Mk 8.38). Thus by this attribute the risen Christian is shown to share the innermost secret of power of the divinity and its awesomeness.

The fourth property is difficult to evaluate: "When it is sown it embodies the soul, when it is raised it embodies the spirit" or literally "it is sown a physical body, it is raised a spiritual body". By the former alternative Paul means the natural life by which Adam

28

"became a living soul" (2 Cor 25.45, quoting Genesis 2.7); by the latter he means the heavenly life of the new age when man is possessed by the Spirit of God. In all this Paul's interest is primarily in the resurrection body of the Christian, how the Christian will be in the resurrection. But since the risen Christian is to be modelled on Christ who is the first-fruits of all who have fallen asleep, everything he says applies *a fortiori* to the risen Christ. This will be important when we come to consider the gospel narratives of the risen Christ.

c) *The New Spirit*

There is, however, a certain sense in which the Christian has already begun to share in the transformation of the resurrection. Although our "wretched bodies" have not yet been transformed, our participation in Christ's body, which is a risen body, means that we share his Spirit, and that his Spirit is at work in us as the life-principle already informing us. It is in this way that we already participate in the new, eschatological age. The resurrection of Christ has released the Spirit. He has become a life-*giving* Spirit (1 Cor 15.45).

The idea was very strong in Judaism that the gift of a new Spirit would be the centre of the renewal of the world which God would accomplish at the time of the Messiah. Most graphic of many passages is Ezekiel's description of the valley of the dead bones: vast quantities of whitened bones, representing the scattered and arid remains of God's people, would miraculously rise to new life as God breathed his Spirit upon them, in a new way from that in which he breathed life into Adam who "became a living soul". The opening motif of Peter's speech at Pentecost is that this dawning of the eschatological age has occurred in the outpouring of the Spirit upon the apostles: "This is what the prophet spoke of "In the days to come — it is the Lord who speaks — I will pour out my spirit on all mankind" (Acts 2.16-17, quoting the prophet Joel).

Indeed, in the community of the New Testament the activity of the Spirit seems to have been a basic datum of experience, to be seen in their extraordinary life and their new powers. So obvious was it that Paul can appeal to it when he is writing to the Galatians as an obvious phenomenon which demands explanation as something wholly new to Judaism: "Does God give you the Spirit so freely and work miracles among you because you practise the law, or because you believed so freely what was preached to you?" (Gal 3.5). Paul himself claims that Christ is in his own apostolate "using what I have said and done, by the power of signs and wonders, by the power of the holy Spirit" converting the pagans (Rom 15.18-19), and under duress proves his apostolic warrant by "all the things that mark the true apostle . . . the signs, the marvels, the miracles (2 Cor 12.12). The latter half of the first letter to the Corinthians is very largely taken up with the regulation of the manifestations of the activity of the Spirit which were occurring in the community at Corinth. These seem to have been widespread throughout the community, some dramatic like healing, speaking in tongues and interpreting prophecy, some less dramatic evidences of Christian community living such as teaching, administration, or even — undramatic, but nevertheless often a proof of the presence in a community of no ordinary spirit — merely of love and consideration.

d) *Conclusion*

In the middle period, then, when Paul is writing the Great Epistles, he concentrates, in his thinking on the resurrection, on its effect on the Christian. His concern is always with the flock to whom he is writing and the effect of the saving mysteries for them. For them the chief ways in which he expresses the effects of the resurrection are in the present outpouring of Christ's spirit and in the future hope of transformation and transfer into the sphere of the divine. Both these are really aspects of his teaching on the body of Christ, according to which Christians are now identified with Christ by being baptised into him and by sharing his life-principle which is the Spirit. For the risen Christ himself the corollaries are that as the first-fruits from the dead he is both source of the Spirit which informs Christians and the pledge of their future transformation in the resurrection. It is significant that there is as yet no reflection on the risen Christ and his position for its own sake. As in Thessalonians he was thought of principally as leader in the triumphal procession, and it was only incidental that terms were used which suggest that his position is divine, so in the teaching on the risen Christ in the Great Epistles he is envisaged above all as the source of the Spirit for Christians. It is again only incidental that the reader who knows his Old Testament cannot be unaware that in the Old Testament it is the Spirit of the Lord which is to be poured out, whereas the fulfilment of this is the outpouring of the Spirit of Christ. Christ has, seemingly unreflectively, been given the place which belongs to God.


## 5 — THE CAPTIVITY EPISTLES

a) *Authorship*

In the teaching on the risen Christ in Ephesians and Colossians all this has been reversed. The position of Christ has been attacked and the author is concerned to explain what his true position is. The effect of the resurrection on Christians now becomes secondary, and primary is Christ's own position. Whether the author is Paul or not is a question which need not concern us. There are literary problems, and to a much lesser extent theological ones, which have led a number of scholars to deny the Pauline authorship of these letters. But, as we shall see, there is also a marked continuity of thought, to the extent that it is at least equally possible to hold that the differences are best accounted for as developments in Paul's own thinking. Indeed; if it is not Paul himself who is writing it is a religious genius of similar stature as well as remarkably similar cast of mind. Thus the question of authorship needs to be raised only if an investigation is being confined purely and strictly to the thought of Paul. Since our investigation is not so confined, the question is unimportant, and for the sake of simplicity we shall refer to the author of these letters as Paul.

b) *Paul's opponents*

It was a view of Christ current among the communities to which Paul wrote these two letters that led Paul to formulate the view of the risen Christ which he here expresses. To a certain extent one can reconstruct what this opposing view was from remarks which he makes in the letters. There seem to have been two main thrusts of his opponents' doctrine. The first, which concerns us less, was that Christians should continue to observe the Jewish Law in matters of Sabbaths, New Moon festivals and the rules of ritual purity (Col 2.14,16). The second, which is more relevant, was that Christ is only one of many mediators between God and man. In the Jewish tradition at that time angels were becoming increasingly important, and this was connected with the thrust towards observance of the Law, for it was held that the Law was given by angels. The attempt may well have been to put forward the view that Christ, with a new interpretation of the Law, was but another angel. Certainly Paul castigates people "who like grovelling to angels and worshipping them" (Col 2.18). But the stress on the subjection to Christ of Sovereignties and Powers (Col 1.14, 2.10) suggests that his opponents were also influenced by the popular stoic philosophy which attributed a superhuman, personal status to these entities — also called "principles" or "elements" of the world (Col 2.20) — and considered them to be semi-divine mediators between God and the world. It is not possible, at any rate within the compass of this investigation, to go more deeply into the doctrines which Paul is opposing. Even if Paul does not misrepresent his opponents, he takes no pains to give a full account of their teaching. They are, in any case, important to us only as the stimulus to his reply.

## c) *The Resurrection*

In his earlier letters, as we have seen, Paul viewed Christ as the Second Adam, the founder and progenitor through his resurrection of a new humanity. Now he goes further. The great hymn of Christ at the beginning of Colossians falls into two parts, the first concerned with Christ's part in creation and the second with his resurrection; the latter cannot be understood without the former. To describe Christ's part in creation Paul draws heavily on the Wisdom literature which appears in the later period of the Old Testament. Here God's activity in creating the world and maintaining it is ascribed to Wisdom, and

33

this figure is described in ever more exalted terms. Wisdom is a power emanating from God, as God's activity in the world, which is somehow differentiated from God, yet by no means independent of or separate from him. A number of poetic images is used in the attempt to convey a carefully balanced impression. Wisdom is "a breath of the power of God" (Wis 7.25), for breath issues from the inmost being and is in continuity with the person from whom it comes, having no existence apart from that person. Wisdom is "a reflection of the eternal light, the untarnished mirror of God's active power" (Wis 7.26), for a reflection of light is the light itself yet indirect, and a mirror gives back only what is put before it, so that the image is the same yet not the same. Wisdom is "the image of his goodness", and in the ancient world an image, representing the original, was often thought to have powers of the original, which is one of the reasons why Israel was forbidden to make images lest they become objects of worship. In the passage immediately preceding, twenty-one epithets (the perfect number) are ascribed to Wisdom in a way which comes near to making Wisdom divine; and yet Wisdom is present in the world, "she pervades and permeates all things" (Wis 7.22-24).

In his hymn of Christ Paul deliberately refers to this description of Wisdom, to show that Christ is this figure of Wisdom: "He is the image of the unseen God" (Col 1.15). He played the part in creation which the Wisdom literature attributed to Wisdom. In the Book of Proverbs Wisdom participated in the creation of the world. The Hebrew texts of the Bible make Wisdom created, but before anything else in the world:

> Yahweh created me when his purpose first unfolded
> before the oldest of his works.

34

> From everlasting I was firmly set
>> from the beginning, before the earth came into being.
> When he laid down the foundations of the earth
> I was at his side, a master-craftsman.
>
> (Prov 8.22-23,29-30)

But it is important, in seeking to rediscover the meaning of Paul's allusions, to know that the near-contemporary Jewish translators of the Bible into Greek had such an exalted view of Wisdom that they rendered the first phrase "God *possessed* me", thus avoiding saying that Wisdom was a created being. There are, however, probably two ways of stating the same thing, for the author obviously intends to put the creation of Wisdom in a completely different class from the rest of God's creative activity. It is to this passage that Paul refers when he says of Christ that he is "the first-born of all creation, for in him were created all things in heaven and on earth . . . Before anything was created, he existed (Col 1.15-16,17). After the refinements reached by the rebuttal of the early Christological heresies we might cavil and say that the Second Person of the Trinity was generated and not created, but Paul did not have the advantage of that distinction, and in putting Christ in a different class of creation and attributing to him the part in creation played by the divine Wisdom there can be no doubt that he is, to put it in our terms, attributing to Christ the status of divinity. It is, however, perhaps a mistake to force Paul into a straitjacket and seek from him answers to questions which he was not yet ready to reply. Paul's own emphasis is that Christ was the principle of creation for all the world, and its continuing life-principle: "he holds all things in unity" (Col 1.17).

In the second part of the hymn Paul describes the function of Christ as risen:

35

Coláiste Oideachais Mhuire Gan Smal Luimneach

"As he is the Beginning,
he was first to be born from the dead,
so that he should be first in every way,
because God wanted all perfection to be found
    in him"
and all things to be reconciled through him and for
    him" (Col 1.18-20).

The first line of this gives the doctrine already familiar
from 1 Corinthians, that he is the first-fruits from the
dead and the second Adam, the founder and progenitor of a new humanity. But then Paul goes on to con-
centrate more on Christ's own position in himself, as
opposed to his position to benefit those who follow him
in the resurrection. There is a good deal of difficulty
in rendering these lines, and any neat translation
weakens their force and resonance. The expression
translated "be first" is not static as that suggests, but
is an active participle, suggesting continuous activity as
an originating life-principle in every way. And "perfection" also conceals a wealth of meaning. The new-
ness of the new creation to which the risen Christ is
life-principle consists in the reconciliation of all things
through him and for him, or the whole *pleroma*
dwelling in him. The exact sense of *pleroma* is
vigorously disputed, but basically it means 'fullness' or
'completion'. There is a good number of overtones lent
by the use of the word in the popular philosophy
current at the time, according to which God both fills
the world and is filled by it. If this is applied to Christ,
it means that the renewal promised for the end of time
takes place in Christ's resurrection. The renewal was
to be a completion, the fulfilment of God's promises
and the ultimate attainment of the goal of creation.
Christ can be said to fill all things in so far as his re-
creating influence attains to them, and also to be filled
by them, in that their coming under his influence is the

goal of his lordship and so completes him. He restores to the whole of creation the harmony promised by the prophets for the end of time, and his own person is the principle of renewal.

By the time he comes to write to the Ephesians Paul has evolved a new and graphic term to express this function: God planned from eternity to "bring everything together under Christ as head" (Eph 1.10). The term used is *anakephalaiosasthai*. This can be understood to mean that Christ is the new head of the new creation, but the root of the word suggests the more exact meaning of recapitulation, in the sense that putting everything under Christ as principle constitutes a reordering of what was in disorder — the reconciliation mentioned in Colossians. This chimes in also with the development in Colossians and Ephesians of a new terminology with regard to the body of Christ. In 1 Corinthians Paul had taught that Christians are members who together make up the body of Christ. Now in these epistles he teaches that Christ as head stands over against the rest of the body. Formerly Christ was attributed no special single function in the body except that his Spirit animated the whole. But now he is the head and the Church is his body. Again it is a refinement brought about by further reflection on the role of the risen Christ. The Greek word for head can also mean "principle", so that he is called the head for several reasons, not only as principle in the sense of first or leader, making chronological priority, but also as head or principle in the sense of dominion or lordship. Then there is also the sense of logical principle seen in *anakesphalaiosasthai*. In addition, according to contemporary Greek medical opinion, the head was not only the source of wisdom and guidance (as for us the head is the guiding genius of a body) but also the source of nourishment and

37

well-being. Christ, then, nourishes continually as well as guides his body the Church, as "the head by whom the whole body is fitted and jointed together" (Eph 4.16).

So vivid is Paul's sense of the continual nourishment of the body by Christ its head that a considerable development has taken place in his thinking about the risen state of the Christian. In the discussion of the Great Epistles we pointed out (p. 25) that there is a dislocation between Christ who is risen and Christians who are not yet risen; although Christ's life is our life and Christ's life is a risen life, nevertheless all statements about the resurrection of the Christians are in the future. Now in Colossians Paul is so conscious that the Christian already lives with Christ's risen life that he is prepared to say "you have been brought back to true life with Christ . . . you have died and now the life you have is hidden with Christ in God" (Col 3.1,3). Christians are in some sense, it seems, already risen, and this state of affairs is only still to be made manifest: "When Christ is revealed — and he is your life — you too will be revealed in all your glory with him" (Col 3.3). The contrast with Romans is perhaps even more explicit in another passage: "You have been buried with him when you were baptised: and by baptism too you *have been* raised up with him" (Col 2.12). In Colossians at least — it is in a way a more workmanlike letter than the rather formal and florid letter to the Ephesians — this risen life of Christians is very much related to the use of the risen power in their lives, "showing the results in all the good actions you do and increasing your knowledge of God, strengthened, in the measure of his glorious power, never to give in" (Col 1.10). The importance of the risen life which is the life-principle of Christians lies in the power it gives to live according to Christ as head, so that we may grow into him in all ways.

# 6 — CONCLUSION

In the sketch of Paul's view of the resurrection and of the risen Christ one factor will have stood out, a supreme lack of interest in the factual details of the event of the resurrection. His interest is in the present position of Christ and its effect on his followers, not on the means by which he reached that position. One of the puzzling features of Paul's letters throughout their length is his remarkable lack of interest in the history of Jesus. Only once or twice does he quote sayings of the Lord, and he never refers to incidents in the ministry of Jesus. He often encourages the members of his communities to imitate Christ: "in your minds you must be the same as Christ Jesus" (Phil 2.5), but this seems to apply, in his mind, only to the suffering, passion, death and resurrection of Jesus and to the "mind" shown in these. Apart from these there seems to be a total lack of historical interest, and even in these there is a total lack of factual interest. It is only quite by chance that, through the quotation of a piece of traditional kerygma, we learn that Paul's faith or message had the backing of any historical information about the events of Easter. The basis of Paul's own faith and the centre of his interest was clearly his experience of the risen Christ in the community, for it is to this that he appeals again and again, and this that he analyses in his exhortations. It is, however, important to realise that in this paragragh we have made a series of statements about Paul's mind and Paul's Christian faith. For him the experience of the risen, living Christ was far more important than anything to do with the empty tomb, but this fact tells us nothing about the age or reliability of the story of the empty tomb. All we can say is that in the sources, as they have come down to us, interest in the risen Christ in the community precedes all else; but we must add that our one very early source has a peculiarly unhistorical turn of mind. As regards fact, we should add that this one source shows that there was considerable interest in records of factual appearances, though he gives no evidence that there was an interest in a story of the empty tomb. When we turn to the gospels which give us the message of Christ through the story of Jesus it is of course quite a different matter.

---

# INTERLUDE

---

## 1 — HISTORICITY AND THE GOSPELS

Before we approach the actual text of the gospels it is essential to make some preliminary remarks about method, particularly with regard to historicity. In recent years it has become more and more clear that the acceptance of the gospels as documents of their times, written according to the literary conventions of their times and Jewish *milieu,* demands a much more subtle approach to the detailed historicity of events as they are narrated in the gospels than was practised in the exegesis of a few decades ago. It is now recognised — indeed it cannot be denied — that many details of the gospel narrative have found their place there not because the evangelist or his source had any historical recollection of them, but in order to bring out the meaning of an event by means of scriptural allusion;

whether the event actually happened in this way was strictly irrelevant. In Roman Catholic circles this recognition was long delayed through the literalism engendered by the aftermath of the modernist crisis at the beginning of the century. One of the earliest important thrusts towards overcoming it was the authoritative article on Midrash by Renée Bloch published in the *Supplément au Dictionnaire de la Bible* (Vol. 5) in 1957. The principles on which the new method rests — if not yet its detailed application in practice — were approved by a document on the Historicity of the Gospels promulgated by the Pontifical Commission in 1964 [11], and since that time the cautious advance has gathered speed. The most obvious use of the midrashic technique in the gospels occurs in Matthew's infancy narratives, where (as R. Bloch points out) passage after passage is built more upon Old Testament texts than upon factual reminiscence. Many are still surprised or shocked at the claim that this method of composition should be used in the New Testament, and feel betrayed that stories which they once regarded as records of historical fact based on historical reminiscences have in fact no such foundation. It can only be replied that such techniques are constantly used in the later books of the Old Testament, and in the New Testament most obviously in the Letter to the Hebrews and the Book of Revelation, but also by Paul and Acts. There is no inherent reason why such a literary technique, widespread in the contemporary world, should not have been used in the gospel [12]. It is the task of the exegete not to separate the factual content from the interpretation, gather the factual content into his barns and cast all else to the winds, but to search out the

---

[11] *Acta Apostolicae Sedis* 56 (1964), pp. 712-718
[12] A strong plea for treating the resurrection narratives in this way was made by Fergus Kerr O.P., 'Exegesis and Easter', *New Blackfriars* 58, (1977), pp. 108-121

message of the gospel. One stage in this procedure may often be to try to discern what is factual in order to discover what the evangelist's intention was in representing it as he does [13].


## 2 — AN EXAMPLE: "ON THE THIRD DAY"

A preliminary example of just such an enquiry into historicity and theology must be made, before we reach the gospels, with regard to the most primitive kerygma in 1 Corinthians 15.4 "that he was raised to life on the third day in accordance with the scriptures". It has long been a puzzle to know what are the scriptures referred to by "on the third day", and it has been suggested that the reference to the scriptures is directed not specifically to the third day but to the resurrection itself — in which case the temporal clause is otiose and the whole sentence clumsily and ineptly constructed. The most likely passage is Hosea 6.2, "After a day or two he will bring us back to life, on the third day he will raise us and we will live in his presence". The meaning is that the resurrection was to occur in an unexpectedly short time, but the allusion to Hosea also carries the sense that the resurrection is to be, as it is in Hosea, an act of God raising up his people. There are also rabbinic texts, which may well go back to that time, which suggest that God will allow his beloved to remain in distress no more than three days before he raises him from it [14]. Hence the third day denotes a day of salvation and divine rescue from need, and eventually an event of eschatological signifi-

---

[13] An attempt to apply this technique to some important incidents of Old and New Testament was made by the present writer in his *Event and Interpretation* (1973)

[14] K. Lehmann, *Auferweckt am 3. Tag nach der Schrift* (Herder, 1969), p. 262f

cance. It is to this sense of the event rather than to a mere temporal coincidence that the reference to the scripture alludes. Indeed one may doubt whether any temporal reference at all was at first intended, especially since "the third day" is no more exact as a merely temporal reference than our "after a couple of days". The difficulty is increased by the fact that in the earliest narrative, that of Mark, it is not the resurrection which happens on the third day, but the discovery of the empty tomb, an unspecified time after the resurrection has happened. It may well be that the material fixing of the date on the third day is no more than a misunderstanding of a reference which originally had far more import and theological value than a mere statement of date. The earliest Christians did not know when the resurrection itself occurred; it is only Matthew who inserts into the account the event of the great earthquake and the descent of the angel on the morning of the third day. Even this cannot be regarded as the moment of the resurrection, and none of the other gospel accounts have any indication when the resurrection itself happened. All they tell us is that the fact that Christ had risen from the tomb and left it empty was observed on the third day. The resurrection itself could have occurred at any time before this. And yet it soon became an accepted fact in Christian literature, canonised in the creeds, that Christ rose from the dead on the third day. The original sense of the scriptural reference, which commented on the nature of the event, not its timing, was forgotten, and the third day came to be understood in a purely chronological sense.

II.

## THE SYNOPTIC GOSPELS

### 1 — THE ORDER OF COMPOSITION

Before we examine the evidence of the three synoptic gospels about the resurrection, it is essential to make a decision about the order of their composition. Within the compass of this book a position can only be stated not argued, but on the essential points agreement among scholars is so widespread that argument is superfluous. It is now agreed virtually universally that the first of the synoptic gospels to be written was Mark and that Matthew and Luke had the text of Mark before them when they wrote. There is, however, still a good deal of controversy about the relationship of Matthew and Luke to each other and about the sources of the material which they share.

The classic theory is known as the Two-Source Theory. According to this the material shared by Matthew and Luke but absent from Mark is drawn by each of these two evangelists from a collection of Sayings of the Lord which has since been lost. It would obviously be far simpler to do away altogether with this hypothetical collection of sayings, but the adherents of the classical theory maintain that there is no proof of any direct contact between Matthew and Luke (neither of the two knew the other directly), so that any similarities must be due to a third party on which they both draw. One of the classic methods of attack on the Two-Source Theory has been to show that there are significant similarities between Matthew and Luke where they are both editing Mark, which are of such a kind that they can be explained only by direct awareness by one of the two later evangelists of the other's work. Lists of such significant passages have been made by a number of scholars, but the extraordinary fact is that the lists of the principal important opponents of the theory all agree only on one phrase as being significant [1]. It is only about this one phrase (Mt 26.28 and Lk 22.64) that all agree that the similarity between the two gospels can be explained only on the theory that there is direct contact between them. This single instance is surely too slender a basis to destroy the whole of the Two-Source Theory.

More recently, however, a much more serious blow has been dealt to the Two-Source Theory by two books on Matthew and Luke respectively. In his *Midrash and Lection in Matthew* (S.P.C.K., 1974) M.D. Goulder sets out to explain the whole of Matthew without any other source than Mark. He shows that all Matthew's material, both where he is editing Mark and where he is independent of him, is so strongly marked both in theology and method and in style and imagery that it must be ascribed to a single mind in such a way as to exclude any collection of Sayings of the Lord. Similarly for Luke, John Drury's *Tradition and Design in Luke's Gospel* (DLT, 1976) shows that there is no need to

---

[1] *The Synoptic Theory of Xavier Léon-Dufour,* unpublished doctoral thesis by S. McLoughlin (1965), p. 238. A part was published as *Les accords mineurs Mt-Lc contre Mc et le problème synoptique* (ETL 43 (1967), 19-40)

invoke the hypothesis of the collection of Sayings of the Lord, but that the form and content of Luke is perfectly adequately explained by Lukan use of Mark and Matthew, and that many features of the gospel make sense only if Luke was working on and editing Matthew for his own purposes.

It is, as we have said, impossible here to do more than state a position which could be proved only by detailed textual argument. The importance of the thesis is that it shows that Mark's account of the empty tomb is the original one which Matthew edits for his own purposes. Matthew's account was in turn known to Luke, so that when he departs from it we are justified in seeking some reason for his so doing. Perhaps even more important is the fact that it would be consonant with their methods in the composition of the rest of the gospel that neither Matthew nor Luke should be relying for the remainder of their stories of the risen Christ on any other factual source. When they add to and change Mark's account it is not on the whole because they have other factual sources, but because they do not find that the previous account expresses the message of Christ to their complete satisfaction. With regard to the resurrection narratives also, therefore, it should be only with a great deal of hesitation that we attribute any details of the story to a factual source other than Mark to which Matthew or Luke had access.

One further preliminary problem remains, about the extent of the original text of Mark's gospel. The dozen verses which follow Mk 16.8 in most modern texts are so different in approach, style, content and vocabulary from the rest of the gospel that it is impossible to accept that they spring from Mark's pen. Furthermore, the manuscript tradition is divided about them: some of the most ancient and venerable manuscripts omit the whole passage; already the great scholar and historian Eusebius of Caesarea considered them to be inauthentic. A number of manuscripts have verses 9-20; other manuscripts give other short fragments. All the information contained in these fragments can be accounted for as drawn from the other gospels and the Acts of the Apostles, or as fulfilments of the promises made by Jesus during his ministry. The most probable reason for the addition is that later tradition found the ending of Mark at 16.8 to be abrupt and in need of completion. This would particularly seem to be the case to those familiar with the later versions of Matthew and Luke, which did not of course exist at the time Mark wrote. To Mark, however, the ending at 16.8 made perfect and homogeneous sense, so that there was no need to add anything more.

## 2 — MARK

### Mark 16: 1-8

¹ When the sabbath was over, Mary of Magdala, Mary the mother of James, and Salome, bought spices with which to go and anoint him. ² And very early in the morning on the first day of the week they went to the tomb, just as the sun was rising.

³ They had been saying to one another, 'Who will roll away the stone for us from the entrance to the tomb?' ⁴ But when they looked they could see that the stone — which was very big — had already been rolled back. ⁵ On entering the tomb they saw a young man in a white robe seated on the right-hand side, and they were struck with amazement. ⁶ But he said to them, 'There is no need for alarm. You are looking for Jesus of Nazareth, who was crucified: he has risen, he is not here. See, here is the place where they laid him. ⁷ But you must go and tell his disciples and Peter,

"He is going before you to Galilee; it is there you will see him, just as he told you" '. [8] And the women came out and ran away from the tomb because they were frightened out of their wits; and they said nothing to a soul, for they were afraid.

Once it has been granted that the other synoptic evangelists, Matthew and Luke, edit the material they have received by adjusting, expanding and changing what they have received from the traditions handed down in the communities in order to bring out more clearly the message of Jesus, the same must be accepted of Mark. It is of course less easy to see in the case of Mark, because we do not possess the traditions which lay behind his gospel in the same way as we have before us the Markan tradition on which Matthew and Luke were working, and for this reason a reconstruction of what Mark did — and so of the traditions which lay behind him — must be more hypothetical. But the same methods must be used to examine his meaning and intention. The basis of any investigation of Mark's narrative of the empty tomb must be the datum that he stands at a considerably advanced point in the tradition, for he is writing some twenty or thirty years after the first traditional statement of the resurrection (which we found embedded in 1 Corinthians 15) had been in circulation and that the story of the empty tomb had no part in this earliest kerygma which was learnt by heart and handed down. He therefore had considerably greater freedom in his moulding of the material to bring out its message, and also had probably considerably more varied and disparate traditions on which to draw. This is not, of course, to say, as R.H. Fuller says [2], that it is an "ineluctable conclusion" that "the empty tomb is a later legend, introduced by

---

[2] *The Formation of the Resurrection Narratives* (SPCK, 1972), p. 52

D

Mark for the first time into the narrative". The vital question is "into what narrative?", for Mark was the first to compose a written narrative and to weld disparate elements into one story.

It must be admitted that there are difficulties about the story, or in other words, that Mark was not wholly successful in his composition. Firstly the approach of the women is hardly sensible: they come to anoint a three-day-old body, which in the heat of Palestine could be in no condition to be anointed, and it is only when they are approaching the tomb that they think of the patently obvious difficulty of rolling away the stone. There seems, moreover, to be some doubt whether the anointing of bodies for burial was a Palestinian custom at this time, or whether Mark has not rather introduced it from his gentile ambience. These are real difficulties, and were perceived by Matthew, who makes the visit far tidier and more logical by saying that they came merely to visit the tomb, which was a pious Jewish custom of the time, and is compatible with a closed tomb and a three-day-old body. This is, therefore, a minor point in which Mark's reconstruction of what happened (the motive of the women) is unsuccessful.

There is a second strange element in the story, the contradiction of the last two verses, when the women are first given a message and then do not deliver it. On one level one might ask (somewhat facetiously) how anyone ever got to know that the message was given to them; on another level one might more justifiably complain that it is a very unsatisfactory literary process to introduce a message simply in order to cancel it out in this way. The solution is that Mark introduced the message which interrupts the otherwise smooth flow of his narrative because he wanted to refer both backwards and forwards. The reference backwards is to Mk 14.27-28 where, on the way to the Mount of

Olives, Jesus foretells that the shepherd will be struck and the sheep scattered, and that after his resurrection he will go before them into Galilee. Mark wishes to show that this prophecy is being fulfilled and thereby emphasises that even in the darkest moment of his passion Jesus knew what was going on and was in perfect control. There is also a certain prominence given to Peter in both passages. Historically this may well be related to the important place given in the earliest kerygma (as in 1 Cor 15) to an appearance to Peter, for which Mark has otherwise no place. Theologically it is a delicate balancing-piece to Peter's triple denial, showing, in a way much more allusive than the better-known passage in John 21, that Peter has been reinstated to his position of leadership. The mention of Galilee has been variously evaluated, for Galilee has been regarded either as "Galilee of the gentiles" in which case the verse is pregnant with the sense of the mission to the gentiles which is to begin now, after his resurrection. Less probably the prediction that they will see him in Galilee has been regarded as a prediction of the second coming, and a fragile theory has been built up that the early Christians expected the second coming to occur in Galilee and went there to wait for it. Though we cannot, perhaps, now evaluate exactly what Mark meant by his message to the apostles (and, as it was never delivered, we must regard it as a message from Mark to the readers of the gospel rather than at its face value of a message from the angel to Peter and the disciples), but it is safer to connect it with the apostolate which is about to begin. Some additional weight is given to this view by Matthew's gospel, for his last scene in Galilee shows that he understood it in this sense. Indeed it may be said that this verse has the same function for Mark as Matthew's final five verses have in his gospel, and the very awkwardness of its insertion shows the store which Mark set by it. It is in a way the high point of his story of the empty tomb and the purpose of the whole explanation of it.

When these two elements are removed, the inappropriate motivation of the women's visit and the implied message of evangelisation, we are left with a comparatively simple and straightforward narrative. The striking factor about it is that it is in no sense an apologetic story which sets out to prove the emptiness of the tomb. The young man points out the place where he was laid, but there is no indication that the women check or confirm his evidence, as they would have to do if this were the purpose of the story. But in any case it would be a weak apologetic, for the evidence of women carried no legal weight. By the time Mark comes to write his gospel, then, the empty tomb is a datum of the tradition which does not need to be emphatically affirmed. It needs only to be interpreted.

This is in fact what Mark's narrative does, and by a method which is a stock convention in Jewish literature of the time. The young man in white is the sort of heavenly being known as an *angelus interpres*, a heavenly mouthpiece for a divine message. In contemporary and near-contemporary Jewish literature such a method of conveying the divine sense of an event or a phenomenon is a commonplace and occasions no surprise. The central point is the message, and the messenger is no more than a plastic representation to show the reality of the message [3]. A clear Old Testament use of the convention is in 2 Maccabees 3.33, and in the New Testament it is no doubt the

---

[3] It is perhaps useful to bolster this view with the authority of two consultors of the Pontifical Biblical Commission, who can hardly be accused of rashness or unorthodoxy, P. Benoit in *The Passion and Resurrection of Jesus Christ* (Geoffrey Chapman, 1969), pp. 260-261, and Raymond E. Brown, in *The Virginal Conception and Bodily Resurrection of Jesus* (Herder, 1973), pp. 122-123

explanation of the messengers of the infancy narratives (Mt 1.20; 2.13; Lk 1.11,26). In this instance the unimportance of the messenger compared with the message may be gauged from the fact that Luke simply introduces two messengers (to strengthen the testimony) instead of Mark's one. The whole scene is cast in a conventional mode, in that the young man is wearing a white garment which is the conventional garb of a heavenly messenger, and the reaction of the women is similarly conventional: they are stunned by amazement and tremble with fear; it is the stock reaction to a heavenly visitation. Their silence also is part of this reaction of terror and awe before the divine.

The message which this part of the story conveys is, therefore, that the empty tomb is the work of God; it is no human phenomenon, but the hand of God is at work. The climax of the message is, in Mark's addition, the instructions about Galilee; but the climax of the narrative as a whole is the note of awe on which it ends. It is a mysterious and open-ended conclusion which is, in the manner of some modern novels, deliberately inconclusive, leaving the impression that God's power is at work in the world, mysterious and awesome, that the power of the risen Christ precedes his disciples into Galilee, ready for their task as shepherds in the evangelisation of the world.


### 3 — MATTHEW

a) *The Empty Tomb*

Matthew 28: 1-10

   [1] After the sabbath, and towards dawn on the first day of the week, Mary of Magdala and the other Mary went to visit the sepulchre. [2] And all at once there

was a violent earthquake, for the angel of the Lord, descending from heaven, came and rolled away the stone and sat on it. [3] His face was like lightning, his robe white as snow. [4] The guards were so shaken, so frightened of him, that they were like dead men. [5] But the angel spoke; and he said to the women, 'There is no need for you to be afraid. I know you are looking for Jesus, who was crucified. [6] He is not here, for he has risen, as he said he would. Come and see the place where he lay, [7] then go quickly and tell his disciples, "He has risen from the dead and now he is going before you to Galilee; it is there you will see him". Now I have told you'. [8] Filled with awe and great joy the women came quickly away from the tomb and ran to tell the disciples.

[9] And there, coming to meet them, was Jesus. 'Greetings', he said. And the women came up to him and, falling down before him, clasped his feet. [10] Then Jesus said to them, 'Do not be afraid; go and tell my brothers that they must leave for Galilee; they will see me there'.

The account of the empty tomb given by Matthew is an excellent example of the way in which Matthew edits and expands his source, Mark. The distinguished Belgian exegete F. Neirynck has studied in detail the verbal and other changes which Matthew makes, showing how consistent they are with Matthew's own approach and terminology, and concluding that the passage "does not presuppose any other gospel tradition than Mark 16.1-8" [4]. There are nevertheless three important differences from Mark, the guards, the earthquake and the appearance of Jesus to the women.

It has usually been held that the story of the guards is a piece of apologetic to discredit the story, which

---

[4] "Les Femmes au Tombeau: Etude de la rédaction Matthéenne" (NTS 15, 1969), pp. 168-190

Matthew says is still current among the Jews, that the disciples stole away the body. But the most puzzling feature of it is the transparent idiocy of the excuse given by the guards, that the body was stolen while they slept; for if they were asleep when the body disappeared, it was equally possible that Jesus rose from the dead as the disciples claimed. It is hardly surprising that the story has been ridiculed from that day to this, and surely totally implausible that such a tale could have acquired currency among the opponents of Christianity. The point is perhaps not of major importance, but recently M.D. Goulder has pointed out that there is no other instance in the gospel where Matthew has invented or accepted legends without basis in tradition or scripture [5], whereas it is a fairly usual process for him to form little incidents on the basis of scripture (e.g., the infancy stories, the death of Judas). Goulder suggests attractively that the whole incident of the sealing of the tomb and the guards is built upon two passages of the Old Testament of which it is seen to be the fulfilment, Daniel 6 and Joshua 10. In the former, Daniel is thrown into the lions' den which is intended to be his tomb, but from which he emerges unscathed to vindication and honour, "a stone was then brought and laid over the mouth of the pit, and the king sealed it with his own signet" (Dan 6.17). The guards themselves come from a somewhat similar scene, when Joshua has captured the King of Jerusalem and others and imprisoned them in a cave with the order, "Roll great stones to the mouth of the cave and set men there to keep guard" (Josh 10.18). The possibility of such a derivation of the incident is attractive, though hypothetical; even such combining of passages of scripture is characteristic of Matthew's method.

---

[5] *Midrash and Lection in Matthew*, p. 447.

The earthquake which accompanies the descent of the angel and the opening of the tomb in Matthew need not detain us long, for it is typical of the evangelist. He inserts this word almost casually into the account of the storm on the lake (Mt 8.24), and much more significantly recounts an earthquake at the crucifixion (27.51). In this latter instance, as at the opening of the tomb, it is a conventional Jewish sign of the intervention of God, or more particularly his eschatological intervention, a sign that the last times, foretold in such language by the prophets, have arrived.

Much more controversial is the third element of Matthew's additions to Mark's account of the empty tomb, the appearance of Jesus to the women. There is an obvious similarity here with the account of the meeting between the risen Christ and Mary Magdalen given by John. The language of Matthew's passage is entirely typical of him, but the detail that they "clasped his feet" (28.9) is reminiscent of the far more prominent feature of Mary clinging to Jesus in John's story. Moreover it has been maintained that the passage has so little sense in Matthew — being merely a reduplication of the message of the angel — that it must be inserted because it was derived from a separate tradition. Thus P. Benoit, in a famous article [6], held that the Johannine account was the most primitive of all the resurrection stories, and that Matthew's story of the meeting between Jesus and the two women was derived from it. Neirynck, however, has rebutted this claim, showing that the Matthaean incident is an expansion, in the typically Matthaean manner, of Mark's narrative. The incident is certainly to some extent a reduplication, for there is the same counsel from Jesus as from the angel not to be afraid, and a very similar message about seeing the risen Christ

[6] "Marie-Madelène et les disciples au tombeau" in BZNW 26 (1960), pp. 141-152

in Galilee. But the message of Jesus has one element which is lacking from that of the angel, an explicit command to go into Galilee, and this is typical of Matthew. With his somewhat legalistic mind he is often careful to establish an exact correspondence between command and execution, and in fact in Matthew the women run off to give the message which in Mark they never delivered. Matthew carefully records at the beginning of his final scene that the disciples do carry out the order given to them through the women, "Meanwhile the eleven disciples set out for Galilee" (28.16). The only notable similarity with the Johannine story which then remains unexplained is the clasping of Jesus' feet by the women, and this in turn can be explained as part of a formal act of homage, as when the woman of Shunem does homage to Elisha when he has raised her son from the dead (2 Kgs 4.37). The purpose of this expansion, therefore, is no more than to prepare more explicitly and more emphatically for the final scene of Matthew's gospel.

## b) *The Final Commission*

Matthew 28 : 16-20

[16] Meanwhile the eleven disciples set out for Galilee, to the mountain where Jesus had arranged to meet them. [17] When they saw him they fell down before him, though some hesitated. [18] Jesus came up and spoke to them. He said, 'All authority in heaven and on earth has been given to me. [19] Go, therefore, make disciples of all the nations; baptise them in the name of the Father and of the Son and of the Holy Spirit, [20] and teach them to observe all the commands I gave you. And know that I am with you always; yes, to the end of time'.

The last scene of the gospel, set on the mountain in Galilee, is a fitting climax to the whole gospel. It is clearly the composition of the evangelist himself, full of his own stylistic characteristics and a vocabulary which is typical of him alone. The theological themes too are proper to Matthew, and the whole method of composition such that it would be superfluous to postulate any factual source peculiar to the evangelist himself. Two motifs dominate the passage, each of which has been foreshadowed in the gospel.

The risen Christ speaks in the power of universal sovereignty which has been given to him by the Father. In typically Matthaean manner this is expressed by open allusion to the son-of-man scene in Daniel 7, where "one like a son of man" comes to the throne of God and is given

"sovereignty, glory and kingship,
and men of all peoples, nations and languages became his servants.
His sovereignty is an eternal sovereignty
which shall never pass away" (Dan 7.14).

This figure like a son of man represented "the people of the saints of the Most High" (Dan 7.27), and the risen Christ is now represented as being that figure, the new Israel in glory. But whereas in Daniel all earthly power was conferred, in Matthew all authority in heaven too belongs to the risen Christ. This final break-through into power and glory has, as we have said, been foreshadowed in the gospel, for the majesty of Jesus, in contrast to the simple, human Jesus of Mark, has been one of the features of Matthew's representation of Jesus; he has already been looking forward to and thinking of the majesty of the risen Christ.

It is specifically in virtue of this power that Christ sends out his disciples to make all nations disciples. His power will go with them, for, as he says finally, "I am with you always, to the end of time". This presence of Christ arches over the whole gospel, for it echoes the first scene, when the name to be given him is "God-with-us", and a number of other intervening passages, such as "When two or three meet in my name, I shall be there with them" (18.20).

It is, then, in this passage that we learn fully what the resurrection meant for Matthew, since the scene of the empty tomb was only an impetus towards this scene. It means that Christ is always present in his people and is doing his work among them in power. It is much the same message as is expressed by Paul in different terms, through his theology of the Body of Christ and the presence of the Spirit of Christ at work in the Christian. But in Matthew the permanent message is linked much more closely to the single event of the resurrection from the tomb. There are, as we shall see in the last section, many who would accept the permanent message while refusing to link it with resurrection from the tomb. They would then explain Matthew's account as legend or myth. Whether and in what sense this is acceptable remains to be seen.


## 4 — LUKE

a) *The Empty Tomb*

Luke 24.1-12

   [1] On the first day of the week, at the first sign of dawn, they went to the tomb with the spices they had prepared. [2] They found that the stone had been rolled away from the tomb, [3] but on entering discovered that the body of the Lord Jesus was not there. [4] As they stood there not knowing what to think, two men in brilliant clothes suddenly appeared at their side.

⁵ Terrified, the women lowered their eyes. But the two men said to them, 'Why look among the dead for someone who is alive? ⁶ He is not here; he has risen. Remember what he told you when he was still in Galilee: ⁷ that the Son of Man had to be handed over into the power of sinful men and be crucified, and rise again on the third day'. ⁸ And they remembered his words.

⁹ When the women returned from the tomb they told all this to the Eleven and to all the others. ¹⁰ The women were Mary of Magdala, Joanna, and Mary the mother of Jesus. The other women with them also told the apostles, ¹¹ but this story of theirs seemed pure nonsense, and they did not believe them.

¹² Peter, however, went running to the tomb. He bent down and saw the binding cloths but nothing else; he then went back home, amazed at what had happened.


It is no exaggeration to say that the most instructive single phrase which leads most clearly to an understanding of what the evangelists intend by their resurrection accounts — or at least what they do not intend — comes in Luke 24.6. Matthew's resurrection appearance is in Galilee, where Mark pointed too; but for Luke the resurrection appearances must be in Jerusalem. He was certainly well aware that Mark pointed to a resurrection appearance in Galilee, and probably well aware that Matthew actually described one, and yet he quite deliberately sets his in and around Jerusalem. Nor is it possible to attempt to harmonise the two versions by working out a series of journeys backwards and forwards by the disciples, so that appearances in both localities (a week's journey apart) fit together. This attempt would be misconceived, for Lk 24.6 shows it to be contrary to Luke's mind; in the perfect knowledge of the signpost towards Galilee contained in the angel's words in Mark, he deliberately removes it to accord with his own plan, and changes the words slightly but significantly. In Mark he read "He will go before you *into Galilee* there you will see him *as he said to you*". This he deliberately changes to make the reference to Galilee past not future, "Remember *what he said to you* while he was still *in Galilee*". He also removes the passage on the way to the Mount of Olives when Jesus made the prophecy of going before them into Galilee (Mk 14.28), though he makes no attempt to provide any clear reference to the new phrase "what he said to you while he was still in Galilee"; there is no clear reference to the resurrection in Luke's version of the Galilean ministry.

Now Luke's preference for Jerusalem as the scene of the resurrection appearances is a function of his whole geographical schema. The gospel begins and ends in Jerusalem, and the final journey to Jerusalem is given an importance by Luke which it enjoys in none of the other gospels, occupying as it does well over half the space given up to the ministry of Jesus, containing the vast majority of his teachings in Luke, and inaugurated by a solemn declaration of Jesus' intention to go up to Jerusalem. By reverse motion, the message of Jesus in the Acts of the Apostles spreads in ever widening circles from Jerusalem, but remains always in contact with the mother-church at Jerusalem. Clearly Jerusalem plays a most important part for Luke, and so he considers it fitting that he should narrate the resurrection appearances there, at the pivot of the gospel.

But what is so highly instructive is his method of operating the transfer. One is tempted at first to suppose merely that from the stock of many stories current Luke chose to tell those which concerned the environs of Jerusalem rather than Galilee. But the change which he makes to Mark's account of the angel's words shows that he is deliberately suppressing the Galilee stories. The small falsification of history at Lk 24.6 — for so it must appear to a modern reader — leads one to suspect a larger falsification of history. Indeed it suggests, and here the crucial point is reached, that to the evangelist the historicity (in the modern sense of that word) of his resurrection stories is unimportant. We have already seen in the consideration of Matthew's account that he introduces small incidents such as the earthquake; almost certainly the meeting of the women with Jesus has no other factual basis than a desire to clarify and emphasise the order to move into Galilee in preparation for the final scene on the mountain. That scene itself is not of such a kind as to suggest that any factual reminiscence lies behind it; it is simply that Matthew sees it to be the entirely appropriate conclusion of the gospel and prelude to the evangelisation of the world.

In his turn it is obvious that Luke makes minor adjustments to the account of the empty tomb. He is the first to make the story an apologetic one by stating explicitly that the women "could not find the body of the Lord Jesus" (24.3), thus implying that they searched for it and registered for themselves — by contrast to the women in Mark and Matthew, who do not check for themselves but rely on the angel's word — that the tomb was empty. He introduces a second angelic messenger, perhaps to strengthen the force of the angelic testimony by putting it in the mouth of two witnesses. He also introduces into the message a foretaste of the kerygmatic proclamation which will become standard — and in the same language — in the missionary preaching of the Acts, and already in the preaching of the risen Lord on the way to Emmaus. Thus he makes the finding of the tomb empty the beginning of the Christian mission. Finally the apologetic motif is strengthened by the disbelief of the apostles to whom the women deliver the message, and still further by the incident in which

Peter goes to the tomb, finds the grave-clothes and comes away not in belief but simply in wonder and amazement [7].


b) *The Road to Emmaus*

Luke 24.13-35

[13] That very same day two of them were on their way to a village called Emmaus, seven miles from Jerusalem, [14] and they were talking together about all that had happened. [15] Now as they talked this over, Jesus himself came up and walked by their side; [16] but something prevented them from recognising him. [17] He said to them, 'What matters are you discussing as you walk along?' They stopped short, their faces downcast.

[18] Then one of them, called Cleopas, answered him, 'You must be the only person staying in Jerusalem who does not know the things that have been happening there these last few days'. [19] 'What things?' he asked. 'All about Jesus of Nazareth' they answered 'who proved he was a great prophet by the things he said and did in the sight of God and of the whole people: [20] and how our chief priests and our leaders handed him over to be sentenced to death, and had him crucified. [21] Our own hope had been that he would be the one to set Israel free. And this is not all: two whole days have gone by since it all happened; [22] and some women from our group have astounded us; they went to the tomb in the early morn-

---

[7] A number of commentators reject this incident as inauthentic to Luke and derived from the closely parallel incident in Jn 20.3-10. A few manuscripts, in the Western manuscript tradition, omit it from the text of Luke. But the overwhelming testimony of the manuscripts is behind it, and a spirited and entirely convincing defence of it has been made by M.-E. Boismard, *Synopse des Quatre Evangiles*, Vol. 2 (Le Cerf, Paris, 1972), pp. 445-446

ing, [23] and when they did not find the body, they came back to tell us they had seen a vision of angels who declared he was alive. [24] Some of our friends went to the tomb and found everything exactly as the women had reported, but of him they saw nothing'.

[25] Then he said to them, 'You foolish men! So slow to believe the full message of the prophets! [26] Was it not ordained that the Christ should suffer and so enter into his glory?' [27] Then, starting with Moses and going through all the prophets, he explained to them the passages throughout the scriptures that were about himself.

[28] When they drew near to the village to which they were going, he made as if to go on; [29] but they pressed him to stay with them. 'It is nearly evening' they said 'and the day is almost over'. So he went in to stay with them. [30] Now while he was with them at table, he took the bread and said the blessing; then he broke it and handed it to them. [31] And their eyes were opened and they recognised him; but he had vanished from their sight. [32] Then they said to each other, 'Did not our hearts burn within us as he talked to us on the road and explained the scriptures to us?' [33] They set out that instant and returned to Jerusalem. There they found the Eleven assembled together with their companions, [34] who said to them, 'Yes, it is true. The Lord has risen and has appeared to Simon'. [35] Then they told their story of what had happened on the road and how they had recognised him at the breaking of bread.

It is not, however, only minor adjustments that are at stake, but even such a large incident as the disciples on the road to Emmaus. This story is thoroughly Lukan in style, thought and vocabulary, betraying no element which could not have originated with him. For the style and vocabulary the study may easily and convincingly be undertaken by the use of a concordance. For the thought it may suffice to show that any number of Lukan interests, many of which we have already remarked, are at play. There is the initial doubt and disbelief (24.11-12), the same apologetic interest in proving the physical reality of the risen body (24.2, 39,43, seen here also in the breaking of bread), the same kerygmatic motif of explaining what had happened by reference to the scriptures (24.7 "it was necessary" repeated also in 24.26). Even leaving aside the infancy narratives, we may be sure that Luke composed other stories in his gospel on other bases than factual reminiscence, for example the story of the widow of Naim's son [8], which is certainly composed on the model of the raising of the widow's son by Elijah in 1 Kgs 17.8-24. Also suggestive of Lukan origin is the parallel between the story of the disciples on the road to Emmaus and the story of Philip and the Ethiopian in Acts 8.26-40. None of these indications amounts to proof that Luke created the story; it remains possible, but by no means necessary, that there is some factual basis for it which Luke has thoroughly transformed and shaped into his own idiom in order to teach his own lessons. Furthermore, lest it should appear that doubt cast on this story necessarily carries with it doubt also about the historical actuality of the finding of the tomb empty, it must be pointed out that the two stories are of a completely different literary type, the story of the road to Emmaus being an extended and polished literary composition, the story of the empty tomb a much more primitive and laboured fragment.

Whatever its origin, this story plays a crucial part in Luke's resurrection narrative. Before now everyone has disbelieved the reality of the resurrection, and this

[8] J. Drury, *Tradition and Design in Luke's Gospel*, p. 71

E

attitude is exemplified to the full in the first half of the story, in which the disciples fail to recognise Jesus. But from the second half onwards the risen Christ is recognised by his disciples, not only in this story but in the incidents which follow. It is, therefore, the turning-point in the narrative, and for this reason holds the predominant and central position among all the incidents. In itself also it is built on a carefully balanced plan, setting off from and arriving back at Jerusalem, beginning with Jesus' approach and ending after his departure, their failure to recognise him being their first reaction and successful recognition their last. The central point, between these extremes, is the two-stage process by which they are led from incomprehension to understanding. First Jesus explains to them the meaning of his suffering from the scriptures, showing how it was decreed by the Father. This does not suffice to bring them understanding, but does bring them nearer: they had been "so slow to believe", but then they say their hearts were burning within them. The final stage, however, is reached only at the breaking of bread, and it is at this point that their eyes are opened. Luke's message is, therefore, wider than the immediate context of the resurrection narratives, envisaging also the more developed Christian community; it teaches that the eucharistic celebration, which was preceded by the explanation of the scriptures in Christological sense, is the *locus* where Christ is recognised and greeted by his own.

c) *Appearance at Jerusalem*

Luke 24.36-49

[36] They were still talking about all this when he himself stood among them and said to them, 'Peace

be with you!' [37] In a state of alarm and fright, they thought they were seeing a ghost. [38] But he said, 'Why are you so agitated, and why are these doubts arising in your hearts? [39] Look at my hands and feet; yes, it is I indeed.

Touch me and see for yourselves; a ghost has no flesh and bones as you can see I have'. [40] And as he said this he showed them his hands and feet. [41] Their joy was so great that they still could not believe it, and they stood there dumbfounded; so he said to them, 'Have you anything here to eat?' [42] And they offered him a piece of grilled fish, which he took and ate before their eyes.

[44] Then he told them, 'This is what I meant when I said, while I was still with you, that everything written about me in the Law of Moses, in the Prophets and in the Psalms, has to be fulfilled'. [45] He then opened their minds to understand the scriptures, [46] and he said to them, 'So you see how it is written that the Christ would suffer and on the third day rise from the dead, [47] and that, in his name, repentance for the forgiveness of sins would be preached to all nations, beginning from Jerusalem. [48] You are witnesses to this. [49] And now I am sending down to you what the Father has promised. Stay in the city then, until you are clothed with the power from on high'.

Now that the recognition of Jesus has occurred Luke builds on it with a story of the apparition of Jesus at Jerusalem. The fact that it shares some features with John's narrative in Jn 20.19-23 may suggest that both evangelists were drawing on a somewhat shadowy source which they each expand, enlarge, and clarify. The elements which both evangelists share, and which would therefore provide the skeleton of the story, are that Jesus appears to his disciples suddenly, in a closed room at Jerusalem, on the evening of the day the tomb was found empty, insist that they touch his body to provide a proof that it is a real physical body and not a ghostly one, and that Jesus gives his disciples a commission to forgive sins. This would be the bare bones of the recollected story, though one might add the two minor details that Jesus greets them "Peace be with you" (this is a normal enough Jewish greeting, "Shalom", but its omission by some manuscripts of Luke has led scholars to suspect that it has intruded into Luke's text from John) and that the disciples rejoiced (in Luke, curiously, this is given as a reason for their temporary disbelief, in much the same way as their grief at the agony in the garden is given as an excuse for their failure to stay awake. Luke 22.45).

On the other hand it is possible to hold also that John has derived his story from Luke. Certainly some of the Johannine divergences from Luke are easily explicable in the two Johannine versions (20.10-23 and 20.24-29). One oddity is that Jn 20.20 retains the physical proof of the reality of his body, though it has much less point than in Luke, as there is no hint of doubt. The Johannine narrative is skeletal, intended chiefly to support the message — which is undeniably Johannine theology — in the commission which follows. Yet even so John introduces his own particular motif of fear of the Jews, the person of Thomas who comes only in his gospel and in both versions tells them to touch his hands and his *side*. Luke has here hands and *feet*, but the change to *side* is obviously dictated by the highly significant wound to the side in John's crucifixion narrative. The theme of Jesus asking them for something to eat is, in John, transferred from this story to Jn 21.5. There is nothing, therefore, to prevent John's account being derived basically from Luke, and we are then again faced with the problem of the derivation of Luke's story.

John Drury suggests [9] that this incident draws its inspiration from Matthew's stories: Jesus' question in Luke about their agitation and doubt echoes the doubt on the part of some when he appears in Matthew on the mountain. The emphasis on the physical body, and specifically the feet, comes from Matthew's scene when the women fall at Jesus' feet and take hold of them. The mission charge is only Luke's version of the final command in Matthew. The theory is attractive, and may be completed by drawing for other elements on the story of the road to Emmaus (Jesus' first question to them, the fact that he eats with them). It would make the scene a typically Lukan composition, expanding mere suggestions in Matthew in a way which is familiar with him. Certainty is impossible, but it would surely be consistent with what we have seen of the evangelists' methods of composition that the narrative should have been composed in this way.

The difference in the missionary charge from that of Matthew is highly characteristic of the theology of the two evangelists. For Matthew the central point is to make disciples, teaching them to obey Christ's commandments. In continuity with his Jewish background he envisages Christianity very much in terms of obedience to a law, the law of Christ which is the fulfilment and perfection of the Old Law completed by the law of love. For him Jesus is a law giver, giving the principal law, the Sermon on the Mount, from a position seated on a mountain in the same way as Moses. The Christian teacher is a scribe after the manner of the Jewish scribes (Mt 13.52) and the Christian disciple is modelled on the disciples of the rabbis. For Luke, on the other hand, the task of the Christian preacher is to proclaim "repentance for the forgiveness of sins" (24.47). Repentance — or more literally "a change

---

[9] *op. cit.,* p. 128

of heart" — is the purpose and end of the early preaching of the apostles in the Acts. Luke's gospel abounds in passages which stress the mercy and love of God inviting sinners to repentance, and the joy in heaven at the repentance of a single sinner. The centrepiece of the great journey when most of Jesus' teaching occurs is the great parables of repentance, the lost sheep and the lost coin and the prodigal son (better named "the forgiving father") and the conclusion of it is formed by the parable of the repentant tax-collector and finally the story of Zacchaeus. It is, then, hardly surprising that the proclamation of repentance should be, in Luke's view, the primary task entrusted by the risen Christ to his witnesses.

d) *The Final Blessing*

Luke 24.50-53

[50] Then he took them out as far as the outskirts of Bethany, and lifting up his hands he blessed them. [51] Now as he blessed them, he withdrew from them and was carried up to heaven. [52] They worshipped him and then went back to Jerusalem full of joy; [53] and they were continually in the Temple praising God.

The finale of Luke's gospel, as its beginning, is full of Old Testament reminiscences: Jesus blesses his disciples with a high-priestly blessing, after the manner of Simon the High Priest:

Then he would come down and raise his hands
over the whole concourse of the sons of Israel,
to give them the Lord's blessing from his lips.
(Sira 50.20)

Then he is taken from his disciples up to heaven as was Elijah the prophet (2 Kgs 2.11). Again there is the similarity with, yet difference from, Matthew in this final blessing. Luke sets it near Jerusalem and they return to Jerusalem to await the power promised them: Matthew locates the scene in Galilee. Each uses the Old Testament to give the scene the overtones he requires, but each in his own way, just as Matthew brackets the gospel on this occasion by the promise of lasting presence of Christ, so Luke too brackets the gospel: the expression "great joy" has occurred only in the message to the shepherds at Christ's birth; it is fulfilled when the disciples return to Jerusalem "with great joy". Joy in the community and the praise of God are the final effects of Christ's resurrection according to Luke.

## 5 — CONCLUSION

In our examination of the synoptic gospels it has appeared that the only narrative about the resurrection for which the evangelists had a solid basis of detailed fact was the story of the discovery of the empty tomb. This story, first given by Mark, was elaborated successively by Matthew and Luke in order to bring out what they see to be the important truths about the event. There was also, of course, the tradition, already seen in a fragment of traditional catechesis in Paul, of appearances of the risen Lord to Peter, then to the Twelve and then to five hundred of the brethren at once. But of these the synoptists make use of only one, the appearance to the Twelve (or, more accurately, to the Eleven, since Judas was no longer among them), although the special position given to Peter in Mark's angelic message *could* be interpreted as intending some special appearance for him. In their treatment of this appearance the synoptists act with the greatest liberty: Matthew locating it in Galilee and Luke in Jerusalem, although there is good reason to believe that Luke is elaborating Matthew's account for his own theological purposes. Their treatment would be consistent with the handing down of this fragment of catechesis entirely without further details, so that they were free to elaborate it as they felt necessary. The fact that John and Luke have a certain amount of common material in their accounts of the appearance at Jerusalem has been taken by some scholars as an indication that there was a common tradition on which they both depend. But an alternative explanation seems more attractive, that John depends on Luke, and that Luke's account is itself elaborated from certain hints in Matthew's narrative seen in the light of his own theology. It would take an extreme poverty of theological perception to fail to realise that an appearance to the Twelve by the risen Lord must have included some charge or commission for their work of witnessing to him in the world, and in Matthew and Luke this charge echoes exactly, as we have seen, the interpretation of discipleship which is mediated by the two gospels.

About the risen Lord himself each of the evangelists has his own emphasis to add. From the approach of Mark's gospel it is obvious that the empty tomb is a datum of tradition to him, and that his task was to interpret this phenomenon. The main emphasis of his interpretation is that it is no natural happening but the result of an awesome divine intervention. Matthew increases the awesomeness of it by introducing the earthquake, which also serves to show that it is the beginning of the eschatological era. He also insists more strongly on the reality of the resurrection, both by introducing the Jewish legend of the grave-robbery in order to refute it, and by beginning to insist on the physical reality of the body. In Matthew this is little more than a hint provided by the women taking hold of his feet, but in Luke it will become a major pre-occupation, demonstrated in the risen Christ eating with his disciples and offering his body to them to be touched. This is no doubt because Luke, unlike Matthew, was writing in a hellenistic environment. Whereas the Jews could conceive no other form of resurrection (on the last day) than a bodily one in which the whole physical person is involved, to the Greeks the idea of a spirit or soul surviving after the physical death and bodily corruption of a person is a commonplace. Ghost stories were as common among them as they are today. It was, therefore, important for Luke to insist that it was no ghost that they saw (24.37) but a real, physical body.

There is another element which is almost invariable in Matthew's and Luke's appearance stories. Besides the motif of fear and awe before the risen Lord, there is also the motif of hesitation. When Jesus appears on the mountain in Galilee, some do reverence but some hesitate (Mt 28.17). The disciples on the road to Emmaus at first fail to recognise their companion, and when Jesus appears in Jerusalem they are at least upset and discuss with each other (Lk 24.37-38). Two possible explanations of this may be given. Either the lesson may be apologetic; obviously the deeper the unwillingness to accept, the more convincing the proof must have been when at last it is accepted; the hesitation would then act as a reassurance to the reader to believe in the reality of the physical body. Or the lesson may be more theological, connected with an aspect of the resurrection which featured largely in Paul's teaching in 1 Corinthians (p. 26): the risen body is somehow transformed. It would seem that the transformation is such — and this feature re-appears again in the Johannine stories — that the risen Lord is not easily or not immediately recognisable. Analogy may be some help here: if one has known a friend only in one particular frame of mind (e.g., morose, or tortured with the pain of physical illness), one might fail to recognise the same friend in a totally different state (transfigured by the joy of falling in love, or healthy and recovered from illness). Or, lest it might seem that we are suggesting that Jesus was always miserable or tortured during his earthly life, if one knows a member of the family only within the intimate and informal warmth of the family, one might temporarily have difficulty in recognising the same member of the family acting in the official and formal capacity of managing director, judge or captain of a ship. This is no more than an analogy, but it may give some idea which can be applied to the difference between Jesus during his earthly life and after his transformation at the resurrection, transfigured by the awesome authority, power and — in a word — glory of the divine.

# III.

---

# THE GOSPEL OF JOHN

---

*Preliminary*

An acute problem of method confronts us here. The gospel of John is pre-eminently the fruit of meditation and reflection, in which the author does not take pains to distinguish between Jesus during his earthly life and the Christ transformed by his resurrection, so that to some extent it is already the risen Christ whom we hear and see during the earthly ministry. In a curious way the community around Jesus are already the Church, and Jesus is speaking to them already as though he and they were already in the post-resurrection situation. At the same time there is an intense thrust throughout John towards the "hour" of Jesus, which is the moment of his death and resurrection. Two methods of procedure would therefore be possible, either to discuss first the resurrection as it shows in the body of the gospel, and the explicit resurrection accounts only after that, in other words to follow the obvious chronological order; or it would be possible — and this is the method which we will adopt — to follow what is in fact the logical order, by discussing first the accounts of the risen Christ and only then the effects of the resurrection as seen in the narrative of Christ's earthly life.

## 1 — RESURRECTION STORIES

a) *The Empty Tomb*

John 20.1-18

<sup>1</sup> It was very early on the first day of the week and still dark, when Mary of Magdala came to the tomb. She saw that the stone had been moved away from the tomb <sup>2</sup> and came running to Simon Peter and the other disciple, the one Jesus loved. 'They have taken the Lord out of the tomb' she said 'and we don't know where they have put him'.

<sup>3</sup> So Peter set out with the other disciple to go to the tomb. <sup>4</sup> They ran together, but the other disciple, running faster than Peter, reached the tomb first; <sup>5</sup> he bent down and saw the linen cloths lying on the ground, but did not go in. <sup>6</sup> Simon Peter who was following now came up, went right into the tomb, saw the linen cloths on the ground, <sup>7</sup> and also the cloth that had been over his head; this was not with the linen cloths but rolled up in a place by itself. <sup>8</sup> Then the other disciple who had reached the tomb first also went in; he saw and he believed. <sup>9</sup> Till this moment they had failed to understand the teaching of scripture, that he must rise from the dead. <sup>10</sup> The disciples then went home again.

<sup>11</sup> Meanwhile Mary stayed outside near the tomb, weeping. Then, still weeping, she stooped to look inside, <sup>12</sup> and saw two angels in white sitting where the body of Jesus had been, one at the head, the other at the feet. <sup>13</sup> They said, 'Woman, why are you weeping?' 'They have taken my Lord away' she

replied 'and I don't know where they have put him'.
[14] As she said this she turned round and saw Jesus standing there, though she did not recognise him. [15] Jesus said, 'Woman, why are you weeping? Who are you looking for?' Supposing him to be the gardener, she said, 'Sir, if you have taken him away, tell me where you have put him, and I will go and remove him'. [16] Jesus said, 'Mary!' She knew him then and said to him in Hebrew, 'Rabbuni!' — which means Master. [17] Jesus said to her, 'Do not cling to me, because I have not yet ascended to the Father. But go and find the brothers, and tell them: I am ascending to my Father and your Father, to my God and your God'. [18] So Mary of Magdala went and told the disciples that she had seen the Lord and that he had said these things to her.

There are puzzling features to this narrative, which fall into place only if one is already aware of the synoptic version of the finding of the empty tomb. Firstly, Mary Magdalen's visit to the tomb is unmotivated, and her discovery of *the* stone removed presupposes knowledge by the reader of the story from elsewhere; this verse has all the appearance of a hurried summary, dependent on a fuller account. Secondly Mary's word is significant when she says "*we* don't know where they have put him", as though she were not alone but were in company with others: incidentally, further trace of dependence on another, fuller account is that in John's version she has as yet no means of knowing that the body has gone. These first two verses represent, then, a truncated version of a story such as that given in Mk 16.1-8.

Next comes the story of Peter and the other disciple running to the tomb and finding only the grave clothes. This again becomes luminously clear and functional if it is compared to the story about Peter in Lk 24.12.

In both stories Peter's part is similar, except that in John it is not explicitly stated that he fails to understand, but only implied by the contrast with the other disciple who "saw and believed". This is the second time John has introduced the mysterious "other disciple" into a narrative where in Luke Peter stood alone, the first occasion being in the house of a high priest (Lk 22.25). A good deal of ink has been spilt in an attempt to identify this disciple, the most common suggestion being that it is the author of the gospel, who refrains from identifying himself out of humility on account of the special relationship of love which exists between him and Jesus (it may be assumed that "the other disciple" is the same person as "the disciple whom Jesus loved"). But it is a most attractive suggestion that, rather, than expend energy on the insoluble problem of identification, one should accept his anonymity and facelessness as intentional, and see in this disciple an exemplary and symbolic figure, standing for "the disciple whom Jesus loves" in the collective sense of any faithful disciple of the future. In this case his role in the resurrection story is carefully prepared. At the supper he is characterised by his intimacy with Jesus and the bond of affection which binds him to the Lord, making him the recipient of his secret revelation. In the courtyard of the high priest's house, in contrast to the other disciples who have fled, he is portrayed as faithful to Jesus in his passion, following his Lord in his sufferings, and contrasted even with Peter who denies the Lord. Finally he alone remains at the foot of the cross, standing there over against the figure of Mary, the mother of the Church. If, as has frequently been suggested, Mary here represents the daughter of Sion, the mother of God's chosen people in the Old Testament, the act of Jesus in giving the beloved disciple to be her son shows him clearly to represent the Church, the collectivity of the disciples whom Jesus loves. The importance of this gift is emphasised by the words which follow, "After this, Jesus, knowing that all was now accomplished" (Jn 19.28). It is the climax of Jesus' work on the cross, the climax of his "hour", because it sets the Church on its path by creating the community of love between those he loves.

Considered in this way the beloved disciple takes on additional significance in the resurrection story. It is he who comes to believe at the empty tomb, and who will recognise the risen Lord at the lake (Jn 21.7). The evangelist introduces him to show that faith and understanding are the work of love, born of sensitive awareness and closeness to Christ, rather than of mere seeing. Whatever there was special about the grave clothes (was it that they were still there, when no tomb-robber would have left them behind, or that the position of them indicated that the body had simply passed through them?) John in his version makes no use of them. The perception is born not of rational argument, or Peter might have realised the significance, but is the instinctive realisation of love. This is the lesson which John wishes to teach by introducing "the other disciple", a lesson which has been stressed at intervals throughout the gospel, as when Jesus complains, "You will not believe unless you see signs and portents" (4.48, cf 6.26) and which will be emphasised again at the end of the gospel, "Happy are those who have not seen and yet believe" (20.29).

The third part of John's story of the empty tomb again has Mary Magdalen at the centre of the stage, for her meeting with the supposed gardener. We have already (p. 56) given reasons for thinking that this Johannine narrative is expanded from the Matthaean version of the meeting rather than, as some scholars have proposed, *vice versa*. There are two novelties about the Johannine version, the attractive dramatisation of the incident, and the sayings of Jesus to Mary. It is in the latter that the importance of the passage lies [1]. The saying "Do not cling to me, because I have not yet ascended to the Father" has been explained in all kinds of improbable ways (he was naked: his wounds were still sore). But it is to be seen in the light of Jesus' repeated promise after the last supper, "In a short time you will see me no longer, and then a short time later you will see me again" (Jn 16.16). Jesus is explaining that his glorification is not completed, and that it needs to be completed before he can come to them with the presence which he promised, namely the presence of the Spirit. In contrast to the Acts of the Apostles, with its forty days before the definitive Ascension, Matthew gives no time span before his final blessing and departure, and in the gospel Luke rather awkwardly (for he has to fit in the disciples' journey back from Emmaus in the evening before the Ascension from near Bethany) seems to suggest that the definitive parting is on the day of the resurrection itself. But John makes it clear that the glorification and further appearances are distinct. Although the risen Christ is to appear to the disciples later, the exaltation which plays such an important part in Johannine theology is one movement with the resurrection, all part of his "hour" to which he has been looking forward from the beginning of his ministry, the marriage feast at Cana. When he forbids the Magdalen to cling to him, this is simply a way of underlining that the movement cannot be interrupted. It is also to be seen in function of the same theme as we saw with regard to the beloved disciple: to cling to the earthly, unglorified Christ is the same fault as clinging to sight, to signs and wonders, instead

---

[1] Here, as elsewhere, I am heavily indebted to Raymond E. Brown's *The Gospel according to John* (Chapman, 1971) as must be everyone who now studies that gospel.

of relying on faith. It is an insistence that the way to know Christ is not through flesh but through the Spirit.

The latter part of the saying, "I am ascending to my Father and your Father, to my God and your God" shows that Christ's exaltation takes his followers with him. As a formula it recalls the saying by which Ruth protests that she will enter into complete community with her mother-in-law Naomi: "Your people shall be my people, and your God my God" (Ruth 1.16). It suggests that here too there is to be total community between Christ exalted and his disciples, in accord with his promise at the supper, "I am going to prepare a place for you . . . so that where I am you may be also" (Jn 14.2). It gives this as an intimate part of the reason for his exaltation. There is a plethora of themes here which will be picked up later.

b) *The Appearances in the Upper Room*

John 20.19-29

[19] In the evening of that same day, the first day of the week, the doors were closed in the room where the disciples were, for fear of the Jews. Jesus came and stood among them. He said to them, 'Peace be with you', [20] and showed them his hands and his side. The disciples were filled with joy when they saw the Lord, [21] and he said to them again, 'Peace be with you.

     'As the Father sent me,
       so am I sending you'.

[22] After saying this he breathed on them and said:
     [23] 'Receive the Holy Spirit.
     For those whose sins you forgive,
     they are forgiven;

F

for those whose sins you retain,
they are retained'.

[24] Thomas called the Twin, who was one of he Twelve, was not with them when Jesus came. [25] When the disciples said, 'We have seen the Lord', he answered, 'Unless I see the holes that the nails made in his hands and can put my finger into the holes they made, and unless I can put my hand into his side, I refuse to believe'. [26] Eight days later the disciples were in the house again and Thomas was with them. The doors were closed, but Jesus came in and stood among them. 'Peace be with you' he said. [27] Then he spoke to Thomas, 'Put your finger here; look, here are my hands. Give me your hand; put it into my side. Doubt no longer but believe'. [28] Thomas replied, 'My Lord and my God!' [29] Jesus said to him:

> 'You believe because you can see me.
> Happy are those who have not seen and yet believe'.

We have already suggested that John's narrative here is derived from Luke's account (p. 68) [2]. John's two scenes are so similar in construction that it seems most likely that the evangelist built the second in imitation of the first. But their spirit and themes are totally different from each other; the second is an echo with a different message. The message of the first was the joyful union of Christ with his disciples; alone of the resurrection appearances it remains unclouded by doubt or hesitation. The motif of doubt returns, however, in full force with Thomas. It is as though John has split into two the appearance described in

---

[2] Boismard, *Synopse,* p. 449, maintains that both Luke and John derive independently from an earlier version, closely related to Luke, which he names Proto-Luke. This document is now lost.

Luke in order to bring out more clearly the two themes.

One curious effect is that, since John ends with the confession of faith to which Thomas' doubt gives place, he is compelled to put the missionary charge — which in Matthew and Luke comes right at the end of the gospel — in the penultimate place. The nub of this commission to the apostles is not so much the commission to forgive sins (this may be an allusion to baptism) as the gift of the Spirit. By the word "he breathed on them" there is a deliberate reference to Genesis 2.7, where God breathes the breath of life into Adam and thereby makes him a living being. On the community level there is also surely an allusion to Ezekiel 37.1-14, a prophecy that the people of Israel, represented by dead and dry bones all over the valley of the prophet's vision, will be brought back to life by the new gift of God's Spirit. The last discourse of Jesus after the Supper in Jn 14-17 had been full of the promise of the gift of the Spirit, and now this promise is fulfilled. The risen Christ at last breathes his life-giving Spirit upon the apostles, making them the risen people of God to whom the Spirit gives life and in whose community the Spirit is alive and active. This gift of the Spirit by the risen Christ enables us to rejoin all that Paul taught about the life of the Spirit in the community and in individuals (p. 29).

In the second scene the confession of Thomas forms a fitting conclusion to the gospel (John 21 is an appendix, almost certainly written by another hand; Jn 20.30-31 is obviously intended as a tailpiece to the whole gospel). Here again the end of the gospel forms a bracket with the beginning, for in the whole of the gospels it is only here and in the first verse of John, "The Word was God" [3] that Jesus is explicitly called

---

[3] The periphrasis given by the New English Bible renders the sense more accurately: "What God was, the Word was".

God. That this particular profession of faith should come for the first time after the resurrection raises the whole question of what effect the resurrection had upon Jesus himself. That Jesus assumed the divinity only at the resurrection is an old heresy, long rejected by the Church, and yet some sense must be given to such phrases as that in the Letter to the Hebrews "made perfect by suffering", (Heb 2.10), and Paul's constant stress that it is through the resurrection that he becomes Lord, using "Lord" in a sense equivalent to the Greek translation of the Hebrew divine name. Such questions would require an extended Christological discussion, and here it must suffice to point out that Thomas's is the most explicit and fullest profession of faith which we possess from the New Testament. "My Lord" is a term which fits in with the theology of Paul, even when it is understood to be an echo of the translation of the divine name; but the direct "My God" is without precedent or parallel.

c) *Meeting at the Lake* (*Epilogue*)

John 21.1-23

¹ Later on, Jesus showed himself again to the disciples. It was by the Sea of Tiberias, and it happened like this: ² Simon Peter, Thomas called the Twin, Nathanael from Cana in Galilee, the sons of Zebedee and two more of his disciples were together. ³ Simon Peter said, 'I'm going fishing'. They replied, 'We'll come with you'. They went out and got into the boat but caught nothing that night.

⁴ It was light by now and there stood Jesus on the shore, though the disciples did not realise that it was Jesus. ⁵ Jesus called out, 'Have you caught anything, friends?' And when they answered, 'No', he said, 'Throw the net out to starboard and you'll

find something'. So they dropped the net, and there were so many fish that they could not haul it in. ⁷ The disciple Jesus loved said to Peter, 'It is the Lord'. At these words 'It is the Lord', Simon Peter, who had practically nothing on, wrapped his cloak round him and jumped into the water. ⁸ The other disciples came on in the boat, towing the net and the fish; they were only about a hundred yards from land.

⁹ As soon as they came ashore they saw that there was some bread there, and a charcoal fire with fish cooking on it. ¹⁰ Jesus said, 'Bring some of the fish you have just caught'. ¹¹ Simon Peter went aboard and dragged the net to the shore, full of big fish, one hundred and fifty-three of them; and in spite of there being so many the net was not broken. ¹² Jesus said to them, 'Come and have breakfast'. None of the disciples was bold enough to ask, 'Who are you?'; they knew quite well it was the Lord. ¹³ Jesus then stepped forward, took the bread and gave it to them, and the same with the fish. ¹⁴ This was the third time that Jesus showed himself to the disciples after rising from the dead.

¹⁵ After the meal Jesus said to Simon Peter, 'Simon son of John, do you love me more than these others do?' He answered, 'Yes, Lord, you know I love you'. ¹⁶ Jesus said to him, 'Feed my lambs'. A second time he said to him, 'Simon son of John, do you love me?' He replied, 'Yes, Lord, you know I love you'. Jesus said to him, 'Look after my sheep'. ¹⁷ Then he said to him a third time, 'Simon son of John, do you love me?' and said, 'Lord, you know everything; you know I love you'. Jesus said to him, 'Feed my sheep'.

> ¹⁸ 'I tell you most solemnly,
> when you were young
> you put on your own belt
> and walked where you liked;

but when you grow old
you will stretch out your hands,
and somebody else will put a belt round you
and take you where you would rather not go'.

[19] In these words he indicated the kind of death by which Peter would give glory to God. After this he said, 'Follow me'. [20] Peter turned and saw the disciple Jesus loved following them — the one who had leaned on his breast at the supper and had said to him, 'Lord, who is it that will betray you?' [21] Seeing him, Peter said to Jesus, 'What about him, Lord?' [22] Jesus answered, 'If I want him to stay behind till I come, what does it matter to you? You are to follow me'. [23] The rumour then went out among the brothers that this disciple would not die. Yet Jesus had not said to Peter, 'He will not die', but, 'If I want him to stay behind till I come'.

This chapter bristles with so many problems that it is almost impossible to say anything valuable about it in a short space. Who was its author? How many distinct episodes have been knitted or tacked together? What is the relation of the first part to the miraculous catch of fish in Lk 5.1-11? There is, however, at least a possibility that preserved here is a memory of the appearance to Peter mentioned in the original catechesis preserved in 1 Corinthians 15 as the first of the appearances after the resurrection. The circumstances of the previous hopelessness of Peter, his surprise and the return of the theme of doubt and inability to recognise the risen Christ, all point in this direction and make the scene entirely appropriate for a first appearance but thoroughly inappropriate after the Jerusalem appearances. Additional weight to the likelihood of this appearance to Peter occurring in Galilee is given by the message of the angel in Mk 16.7. The fact that other apostles are present does not preclude the possibility that this should be called an appearance to Peter rather than to the apostles, for the only other disciple who has any prominence is "the disciple whom Jesus loved" who plays the same part in this scene as he did in John's scene with Peter at the tomb. As he was there worked into a scene where Peter originally stood alone, the same is probably true here. (It is, incidentally, in the very last part of this chapter — 21.24 — that this disciple is first identified with the author of the gospel; we can safely say that this runs contrary to the original author's intentions).

The chapter contains much that is of ecclesiastical interest. Until now is preserved the laying of the foundations of the organisation of the Church. Whereas the synoptic gospels have various scenes of importance for Church organisation before the resurrection, John has none. There is no sign of any appointment of the Twelve (Mk 4.13-19 and parallels), or of a promise that they will be fishers of men (Lk 5.1-11). There is no promise of the keys to Peter (Mt 16.16-18), nor that he will strengthen his brothers (Lk 22.32). In John the commission to Peter to be a shepherd comes after the resurrection, as does the breathing on the Twelve which makes them Christ's new community in the Spirit, and now the missionary significance of the catch of fish. The significance of this is that for John the Church is the Church specifically of the risen Christ. Until the risen Christ has breathed on them the Spirit there is no community, no organisation, no leader, and above all no sacraments.

As in the previous incident in the upper room the apostles are, as soon as Christ has breathed his Spirit upon them, given the power to forgive sins which is a hint of baptism, so now there is a hint of the eucharist. One of the most glaring omissions in the gospels is the omission in John of any mention of the eucharist at the last supper, and it has been credibly surmised that this omission is dictated by John's wish to withhold the institution of any sacraments till after the resurrection. There is a good possibility that the meal of the risen Christ with his disciples at the lakeside, when he "took the bread and gave it to them" (21.13) is intended to repair the omission at the last supper. The eucharistic overtones are not, it must be admitted, incontrovertible, but remain no more than a strong possibility. Strength is added by the eucharistic overtones of the meal of the risen Christ with the disciples at Emmaus in Luke, as though it was felt to be fitting that the eucharist which was the centre and source of life to the Church should be represented in the life of the risen Christ with his community.

d) *Conclusions*

In our investigations we have found, then, that the contribution of the Fourth Gospel to the resurrection narratives is more in the field of theology and interpretation than in factual reminiscence. Raymond Brown has given his opinion that "a more biblical approach (than harmonisation) is to suppose that one basic appearance underlies all the main gospel accounts of appearances to the Twelve (Eleven) . . . It makes little sense to construct a series of such appearances to the Twelve; each gospel witness is reporting a slightly different version of an appearance that was constitutive of the Christian community" [4]. The story of the empty tomb seems a firm enough independent unit attested by all the gospels; but for the other incidents, the appearances, the variety of structure and circumstances, and the accommodation of the incidents to the theology of the gospel in which each of

---

[4] *The Gospel according to John,* pp. 972, 973

them occurs, leaves open serious doubt whether the evangelists were doing more than relying on the short original kerygma preserved in 1 Corinthians 15, and elaborating on this and on the work of the previous evangelists in accordance with their own special interests and theologies. One remarkable contribution of John 21 is that he alone provides an appearance which corresponds to the appearance to Peter mentioned in the kerygma of 1 Corinthians. Judgement on the historical correctness of this particular version of it depends on the answer to the seemingly insoluble problem of whether Luke 5.1-11 has transferred to the ministry of Jesus what was originally a resurrection appearance, or John 21.1-13 has made use of what was originally a scene in the earthly ministry to construct an appearance of the risen Christ.

In the field of theology we may perhaps single out, as being of particular importance, two of John's contributions. The first is his stress on the need for the qualities of the beloved disciple in order to acknowledge the risen Christ. Peter does not seize the message of the empty tomb nor recognise the risen Christ at the lakeside; it is the beloved disciple who precedes him in both of these. In spite of his unprecedented profession of faith, Thomas is almost rebuffed by the final saying of Jesus in the main body of the gospel, "You believe because you can see me. Happy are those who have not seen and yet believe" (20.29). John has his sights firmly fixed on believers of the next generation who have no opportunity for physical sight of Jesus.

Consonant with this interest is the ecclesiastical dimension of these chapters, which forms John's second important contribution. For John this period is above all the moment of the founding of the Church. In a way this could be dated to the crucifixion, when as Jesus died he "gave up his spirit" (19.30) — a phrase of deep significance after the promises of the gift of

89

the Spirit which have preceded. But in John's mind the crucifixion and resurrection are but moments within the same "hour", and the gift of the Spirit becomes explicit when the risen Christ breathes it upon the Eleven, thus founding his community. Immediately afterwards he gives them the commission to forgive sins, and in the epilogue he completes the structure of the community by hinting that the apostles are all to be fishers, by giving the office of shepherd to Peter, and perhaps by the eucharistic allusions in the meal at the lakeside. Thus the community of the risen Christ in the Spirit is left fully formed.

## 2 — THE RISEN CHRIST IN HIS MINISTRY

### a) *The Resurrection is Already*

Throughout John's gospel, even before the hour of glorification at the cross and resurrection, it is the risen Christ present to his Church who is depicted. The earthly life of Christ has taken on the colouring of the later state because Christ active in the life of the Church reflects the earthly life of Christ. Through John's method of writing, full of double senses and half-perceived overtones, one receives the impression of the interpenetration of these two spheres, so that the Christ who gives bread to the multitude is already the Bread of Life who will be received in the Church, and the Christ who gives light and faith to the blind man is already the Christ who baptises in the Church. The "hour" of Christ's glory is pre-eminently the hour of his passion, and it is then that his glory shines clearly through. It is the hour of his glorification for which he has been waiting, so that there is no place in John for a transfiguration scene before the humiliation of the passion, for the passion itself is represented as a triumphal procession. His enemies cannot arrest Jesus until he permits it, after they have twice fallen back in awe before him as he pronounces the divine name (Jn 18.5-12 — the Greek expression "It is I" also means "I am", the frequent translation in the Greek Old Testament of the Hebrew divine name). When it comes to carrying the cross, Jesus bears it alone, as a standard of triumph (19.17). Finally, despite the protests of the Jews, Pilate has fixed on the cross the unqualified proclamation, in the three world languages, "Jesus of Nazareth, King of the Jews" — a proclamation to all mankind. Most audaciously of all, the most correct and obvious translation of Jn 19.13 is "Pilate led out Jesus . . . and seated *him* in the place of judgement". Thus in the very moment when he seems to be being condemned, Jesus himself is enthroned as judge and it is the Jews who are being condemned for denying their messianic hopes. Thus for John the triumphant hour of Christ begins, not at the resurrection but at the start of the passion. So, as he prepares for the passion, Jesus prays, "Now, Father, it is time for you to glorify me with that glory I had with you before ever the world was" (17.5). But already before then, at the marriage feast at Cana, "he let his glory be seen" (2.11), and also in his other signs and miracles (12.37-41), though the Jews were blind to it.

The importance of this for our theme is this: just as Christ, already on earth, is suffused with glory, so do his followers, even now, enjoy the effects of the resurrection: "Whoever listens to my words and believes in the one who sent me *has* eternal life; without being brought to judgement he *has* passed from death to life. I tell you most solemnly, the hour will come — in fact *it is here already* — when the dead will hear the voice of the Son of God, and all who

hear it will live" (5.24-25). "Everyone who believes
. . . who eats my flesh and drinks my blood, *has*
eternal life" (6.47,53). The promise is not confined
to the future, but eternal life is already now. In John
the verb "to live" is a typically ambiguous expression,
and Jesus puzzles Martha by saying of her dead brother
Lazarus "Whoever lives and believes in me will never
die" (11.26). At this point Martha, in a typically femi-
nine and practical way, gives up trying to understand
and goes off to get her sister to move the Lord into
action, and bring Lazarus alive out of the tomb, as a
vindication of his words. This is the way in which John
rejoins the Paul of the Captivity Epistles (p. 38), for
whom the Christian is already risen with Christ and
already transformed, living with his risen life. When
Jesus appears in John to be teaching the multitudes or
other listeners, his discourses are in fact addressed to
the reader of a future generation: Jesus speaks as
though after the resurrection, when his glory has been
poured out on them too.


b) *The Promise of the Spirit*


The means of sharing the life of Christ is the Spirit
which the risen Lord breathes on his disciples when
he comes to them in the upper room. But the explanation of what this means comes earlier, in the great
collection of farewell promises for the future which is
the discourse after the last supper. Here John uses the
well-known convention of a parting speech, by a great
leader who is about to die, to the disciples who will
carry on his work, welding this with the hellenistic
convention of conversation at a meal where major
teaching is conveyed. It is almost a refrain of this discourse that Jesus is going away only to return: "I am
going now to prepare a place for you, and after I have

gone and prepared you a place, I shall return to take you with me" (14.3). That this is no promise of a speedy removal from the world is shown by a parallel passage: "I will not leave you orphans; I will come back to you. In a short time the world will no longer see me; but you will see me, because I live and you will live" (14.18). Here the contrast with "the world" (always used by John in a pejorative sense) means that a presence to the disciples is envisaged which the opponents of Christ will not share or realise.

The keynotes of this presence of Christ will be joy ("I shall see you again and your hearts will be full of joy, and that joy no one shall take from you", 16.22; also 11.15; 16.20,21,24; 17.13; 14.28) and understanding of the purposes of God or knowledge of God ("the hour is coming when I shall no longer speak to you in metaphors, but tell you about the Father in plain words", 16.15; also 14.7,20,26; 15.7,15,27; 16.13; 17.3,8,17,26). Perhaps the greatest promise of all is that of friendship: "I shall not call you servants any more, because a servant does not know his master's business; I call you friends, because I have made known to you everything I have learnt from my Father" (15.15). Indeed, after the resurrection this new intimacy and understanding is actually seen operating. Sayings of Jesus which are not understood in their full or correct meaning until the resurrection, then become intelligible, for example, the saying about rebuilding this temple in three days (2.22), or living water (7.39). Nor did they understand the significance of the entry into Jerusalem on a donkey "until Jesus had been glorified" (12.16).

In most of the gospel the agent of this new intimacy with the Father and of Christ's action among his disciples is the Spirit. The Spirit is the means of rebirth by which one enters the kingdom (3.6); it is in the Spirit that man will worship God truly (4.24) and will understand the sayings of Jesus (6.63; 7.39). But in the discourse after the last supper there is a series of sayings which refer to "the Paraclete". In 14.26 the Paraclete is identified with the Holy Spirit, but there is some doubt about the textual accuracy of this ("holy" omitted by some manuscripts); in any case it is methodologically better to see first what is said about the Paraclete before seeking an identification. He is closely connected with Jesus, since the Father sends him in Jesus' name (14.26), at his request, as *another* Paraclete (14.16). This can mean only that he is replacing Jesus, for the whole context is Jesus' imminent departure and his subsequent care for his disciples. He will make clear and remind the disciples of everything which Jesus told them (14.26); and it will be Jesus whom he glorifies because everything he teaches will be from Jesus (16.14).

These sayings suggest that the Paraclete will take the place of Jesus when Jesus has been exalted to the Father. But other sayings insist that Jesus himself will return and remain with his disciples. We are tempted to object that either Jesus is present, or he is absent but the Paraclete does his work for him; it cannot be both simultaneously. The solution lies in a difference in the concept of personality familiar to the Jewish mind. In the Old Testament there are several pairs of figures, the second of which continues the work of the first, takes up his mantle as we say (the current English metaphor is of course drawn from one of these pairs — Elisha with reference to Elijah's mantle). Jesus takes up and completes the work of Moses, is endowed with his spirit, so is often represented in the gospels as a sort of second Moses. Similarly the prophet Malachi (4.5-6) says that Elijah will come again. Jesus says that in John the Baptist he has come (Mt 11.14), and the envoys of the Jewish leaders ask the Baptist directly whether he is Elijah, not merely someone like

Elijah or fulfilling the function of Elijah. It is in the same way that the Paraclete, while being a person in his own right, can also bring the presence of Jesus. In the operation of the Paraclete leading the disciples into all truth John sees Jesus as present. The hour of exaltation is the moment and means of Jesus becoming present in a way which is less confined and more diffused, bringing Jesus' spirit of truth, understanding and love to all his followers.

# WHAT ACTUALLY HAPPENED?

## a) *The Bultmann School*

In *Kerygma and Myth* [1] Rudolf Bultmann wrote: "Christ meets us in the preaching as one crucified and risen. He meets us in the words of preaching and nowhere else. The faith of Easter is just this — faith in the word of preaching". But the current debate on the resurrection seems to spring from a lecture given by Bultmann at Heidelberg in 1960, in which he said "To believe in the Christ present in the kerygma is the meaning of the Easter faith" [2]. The Bultmannian approach was developed in a highly controversial series of lectures given at Munster in 1967/8 by Willi Marxsen. The presupposition behind his investigation, and behind the whole Bultmannian approach, is the characteristically Lutheran position that the more our faith is a leap in the dark, and the less evidence there

[1] Ed. H.W. Bartsch (1948), tr. by R.H. Fuller (Harper, 1961), p. 41

[2] Quoted in C.D.F. Moule (Ed.), *Significance of the Message of the Resurrection* (London, 1967), p. 18

is to make it reasonable, the higher is the quality of that faith. Faith must be founded on the experience of Christ now, as he meets us and seizes hold of us in the preaching, and the so-called faith which relies on the evidence of signs and wonders or any irrelevances of the past, is precisely a barrier to real faith [3]. Clearly, then, the less signs and wonders there are in the New Testament to lead us astray, the less true faith is endangered.

Since, according to this point of view, the evangelists could not have intended to provide us with evidence of signs and wonders (or since if they did so intend, such evidence is at best irrelevant, at worst misleading), the value of the gospel accounts of the resurrection appearances is as so many protestations of faith and of experience of Jesus. The evangelists are, in the enthusiastic sense, testifying, witnessing to their experience of the risen Christ. Moreover, in the New Testament — and on this point of fact rather than of theological principle Marxsen is clearly correct — the statement of belief in Jesus' bodily resurrection is only one possible way among many of expressing faith in his present efficacy and power. In the Letter to the Hebrews the idea does not occur at all, being replaced by that of exaltation or sitting down at the right hand of God; this is also the central concept enshrined in the pre-Pauline hymn in Philippians. In Matthew we find side by side, providing two originally independent and self-sufficient statements of belief, the story of the empty tomb and the saying "All authority in heaven and earth has been given to me". For Marxsen all these are merely expressions of faith, using myth to express what could also be expressed (substituting poetry for myth!) "Still he comes today",[4]

---

[3] W. Marxsen, *The Resurrection of Jesus of Nazareth* (SCM Press, 1970) p. 153

[4] *ibid.*, p. 141

or, even without any explicit reference to Christ in the words of Heinrich Rendtorff on his deathbed, "I shall be safe" [5].

In Marxsen's scheme of things it is essentially the faith which comes first and seeks expression. It is almost by chance that the notion of bodily resurrection becomes the way in which it is expressed. He outlines this process thus:

Someone discovers in a miraculous way that Jesus evokes faith even after his death. He now asks what makes it possible for him to find faith in this way. The reason is that Jesus who died is alive. He did not remain among the dead. But if one wanted to claim that a dead person was alive, then the notion of the resurrection of the dead was ready at hand. So one made use of it. In so doing there was no need to pin oneself down to a particular form of this idea, at least not at the beginning . . . If the idea of the resurrection eventually won the ascendancy, towing the other ideas in its wake, it must not be forgotten that it was a later development [6].

Another expression of the same theory is provided in England by J.A.T. Robinson. In an admittedly popular book [7] he gives a somewhat garish version:

"And then IT happened. It came to them — or rather, as they could only describe it, HE came to them. The life they had known and shared was not buried with him but alive in them. Jesus was not a dead memory but a living presence . . . But the empty tomb is not the resurrection any more than the shell of the cocoon is the butterfly . . . Precisely what happened to the body we shall never know".

There are, it seems to me, three questions raised by such statements, and particularly such statements as

[5] *ibid.*, p. 188
[6] *ibid.*, pp. 138, 147
[7] *But that I can't believe* (Fontana, 1967), pp. 37-40

Marxsen's, concerning the notion of the resurrection of the dead, concerning the evolution of the mode of expression, and concerning the genesis of belief. With regard to the first, it is a dangerous oversimplification to say that "the notion of the resurrection of the dead lay to hand". The notion existed certainly, but the Pharisees envisaged the permanent raising of the dead to unending life only in the general resurrection at the eschaton or end of time.

They knew about the miraculous returns to life, such as that worked by Elijah on the son of the widow (1 Kgs 17.17), and this lay ready to hand for such miracles of Jesus as the raising of Lazarus or the son of the widow of Naim, about whom it is never suggested that their subsequent life was in any way different to their previous existence. But there was no precedent and no expectation of anyone passing individually to the eschatological state predicated of Jesus while the rest of the world went on as before. And this transposition of the idea of the general resurrection to a single individual cannot be passed over so lightly and casually.

Secondly, with regard to the evolution of the mode of expression. It is certainly true that there is a variety of expressions in the New Testament for Christ's state, of which resurrection is only one. But it must be remembered firstly that the earliest kerygma implies at least some sense-experience by "he was seen", and secondly that the derivation of other ideas from the idea of resurrection is logically much easier than movement in other direction. Similarly it is also true that the story of the empty tomb came to us in a later document than the earliest kerygma, but this alone does not argue against an early date for the story, let alone for its unreliability. It has been argued that the absence of the story from 1 Corinthians 15 is a strong argument from silence, that the story was not yet in circulation on the grounds that the story of the empty tomb would have contributed forcefully since Paul is trying to prove the bodily resurrection, but one can see equally well how this story would have obscured the issue, which weakens the argument from silence again. There is simply no means of determining the date of the story, though one influential Catholic scholar, B. van Iersel [8], suggests that it was a story told in explanation of the place when pilgrimage thither had already sprung up.

Thirdly, with regard to the genesis of belief, as C.D.F. Moule points out in his introduction to *The Significance of the Message of the Resurrection* [9], there is a fundamental cleavage between those who hold that the resurrection is the expression of an already existing faith, and those who say it is the cause. But unless the funk of the disciples during the passion, their desertion at his death and their despair afterwards are all highly artificial inventions, some pretty convincing experience was needed to bring them to faith in their master.

The chief support of the Bultmann theory is the conviction that faith does not need, indeed is better off without, any form of bodily resurrection. With this presupposition, their conclusions are hardly unexpected. The existential aspects of this approach are valuable, the stress on the need for a response in faith and the conviction that the meaning of the resurrection is "Still he comes today". But the proponents of this view do not do justice to the conviction of those who first made this response that something marvellous had occurred. That "the life they had known and shared was not ended with him but alive in them. Jesus was not a dead memory but a living presence" (J.A.T. Robinson) was not the sum total of their

---

[8] "The Resurrection of Jesus" in *Concilium* 10.6 (1970), p. 63
[9] See note 3

resurrection faith, or there would have been no need for any reports of appearances or of empty tomb.

b) *And the Bones of Jesus?*

A related and important problem concerns the physical aspect of the resurrection. This problem has been put in various ways. Neville Clarke (in *The Significance of the Message of the Resurrection*, p. 97) says "It is ultimately a matter of indifference as to whether or not the bones of Jesus lie somewhere in Palestine". At first sight this assertion is stunning, for it is a direct contradiction of a naive view of the resurrection. But the position changes when one considers that Jesus was not resuscitated, but rose to new life. There is all the difference in the world between the raising of Lazarus and the raising of Jesus. Clearly Jesus was no longer subject to the normal limitations of human life, nor was his bodily movement so restricted, nor does he seem to have been subject to the normal requirements of nourishment.

Professor Lampe [10] goes so far as to say "I find it difficult to believe that Paul could possibly have believed that Jesus rose from the grave, as or in, a physical body", for he finds it to be incompatible both with what is said about flesh and blood being unable to possess the Kingdom of God and with Paul's statements about transformation at the resurrection of the dead.

A further difficulty is hinted at by P. van Buren: [11] "Because of the influence of the natural sciences, especially biology, on our thinking today, we can no

---

[10] In an interesting radio dialogue, published as G.W.H. Lampe and D.M. MacKinnon, *The Resurrection* (Mowbray, 1966), p 46

[11] *The Secular Meaning of the Gospel* (SCM Press, 1966), p. 127

more silence the questions concerning the changes in cells at death which spring to our mind when we read the Easter story of the Gospels, than we can deny that we live in the twentieth century". It cannot be denied that Jesus' body corrupted, at least partially, for the medical criterion of death is corruption, irreversible damage to the brain-cells, by which their structure changes (corrupts) within two minutes of the cessation of the flow of blood to the brain. If there was not this corruption then we have a case of suspended animation rather than true death. This may be a useful hypothesis for the case of Lazarus, but it is surely superfluous for Jesus' case. Furthermore, as Professor Lampe points out,[12] if Jesus' resurrection is the model of ours, it is essential that his body did corrupt, for ours certainly will, before we are raised again at the resurrection.

Basically, since there is every likelihood that my flesh and bones will corrupt and this will not prevent the resurrection of the body, I see no particular theological problem which would arise if Jesus' flesh and bones underwent the same fate, for this would not interfere with his resurrection in the body. An element in the belief in the resurrection of Jesus is that he underwent "after three days" what his followers will undergo at the end of time, the process by which they enter fully into the eschatological existence. To this corruption in the tomb is no bar. This serves only to emphasise how enigmatic are Paul's statements in 1 Corinthians 15 about the risen body (p. 26), for what a "spiritual body" is we have really no idea. Primarily Paul's doctrine is formulated to show that it is the person who rises again, not just a neo-platonic soul, which in Paul's semitic anthropology cannot be envisaged.

---

[12] *op. cit.*, pp. 58-59

To Paul's teaching we can add only very tentatively from the details of the resurrection narrative that the basic teaching of the physical details such as touching and eating is intended primarily to teach the reality of the body. Touching must be intended to show that the body is really a physical body, and the wounds to emphasise the continuity of this body with the Christ who died on the cross. The implication of entry when the doors are closed is transcendence of the normal barriers of space and time. Eating poses a real problem, since the digestive processes inevitably involve corruption, and perhaps here we may justifiably stop short of literal acceptance.

c) *Conclusions*

There are formidable problems of space and matter involved, and it is perhaps chiefly the failure to accept this fact that has excessively polarised the discussion. There are those who insist that the appearances to Peter, to the Twelve and to the five hundred others were no more than subjective experiences. There are those who attempt to press these appearances as though they must have been meetings like those at a luncheon table or on a station platform. The writers of the New Testament are certainly at pains to show that the risen body of Jesus was a real physical body, for it is to this end that they show the disciples touching Christ, acknowledging his wounds, and giving him boiled fish to eat. But on the other hand the awe which surrounds the experience, the repeated initial failure to recognise the Lord, and perhaps most clearly of all John's careful teaching that an affinity in faith and love is the pre-requisite of recognising the risen Lord — all these show that the experience of meeting the risen

Christ cannot simply be equated with our day-to-day meetings with familiar associates.

The critical Christian will ask, and will ask rightly, whether in this case we are speaking of a wholly subjective experience. Did they merely imagine it? On literary-critical grounds we have granted that the details given in the gospel accounts are very largely expansions and materialisations of a far sketchier tradition which merely express the evangelists' inspired understanding of these events, and which may rest factually on nothing more detailed than the bare recital of appearances recorded by Paul (p. 12). But to the Christian who accepts the New Testament as the gift of God's Word to men, the way simply is not open to say that the evangelists were mistaken in such a way as to mislead us on such an important point as the quality of the resurrection. And if the evangelists teach anything at all about the risen Christ it is that the experience of meeting him was quite different from any experience which might be described as seeing a ghost. Nor it is merely an hallucination brought on by and expressing the conviction that the power of Christ was still present among them. It was not the experience of a ghost and it was not the experience merely of a power or presence in the community.

On the other hand the importance of faith and love in the experience cannot be denied. It might be instructive to ask the evangelists what the experience would have been of those who lacked the qualities of faith and love. At the lakeside the beloved disciple recognised the Lord first, but what would Peter have experienced if he had not been drawn on by the love and faith of the beloved disciple? Nothing at all? The onlookers at Paul's conversion (if we may learn from Luke's account in the Acts) did not enter into Paul's sense-experience of the risen Christ any more than they entered into his conversion; the two are inter-related.

One cannot, for all that, say that Paul's experience was unreal. To say that subjective elements, faith and love, enter into an experience does not mean to say that the experience can be written off as imaginary.

The nub of the matter is that it must have been an experience of a very special kind. At his resurrection Jesus entered into the eschatological sphere. This is one of the important lessons of Mark's story of the empty tomb. The women were experiencing the arrival of the eschaton (this is brought out more fully by Matthew's earthquake). For Jesus this was the completion, accomplishment and exaltation to God's right hand. Just how one is to describe the change brought about by his elevation without detracting from his status as divine during his earthly life is certainly a difficulty, but it is undeniable that at the resurrection he was in some way perfected, and in some way entered more fully into the sphere of the divine. For us, then, the significance of the resurrection is not merely as a proof of Jesus' acceptability with God, or of the reality of his life with us, but as the entrance of humanity for the first time and to an unprecedented degree, in a wholly satisfying and completing way, into the sphere of the divine. The significance of this is that as "first-born from the dead" Christ is the precursor of his disciples. His entrance into the sphere of the divine is the presage of our entrance in his wake. This is why, as Paul says, Christ's resurrection is the basis of all our hope, and "if Christ has not been raised then our preaching is useless and your believing is useless" (1 Cor 15.14).

The quality of the experience is related to the object of experience. Now, if the Christ who was experienced has entered into the sphere of the divine, the eschatological sphere, the new world, then the experience of the risen Christ will be wholly unique. It can be described neither in terms of a meeting on a station platform not in terms of seeing a ghost, nor yet in terms of an inner subjective experience. In 1 Cor 15 Paul has difficulty enough giving any content to the notion of the risen person. He insists that the risen person in the eschatological sphere is a real person and that there is continuity but transformation. But what would be the experience of meeting on earth such a person who had already entered into the eschaton? If we first ask this question we are in a much better position to ask what the disciples' experience of meeting the risen Lord might be expected to be. But at the same time the anguish goes out of the question as soon as one grasps that what the gospel writers are trying to express is precisely this meeting between the historical and the trans-historical, the disciples within history and Jesus already beyond it. This accounts for the stuttering and for the minor contradictions between the narratives; what they try to express is that he remains himself, but is freed from all the limitations of our world.

In this perspective the simplicity of Mark's ending takes on an awesome grandeur. The final message of the young man is one of boundless hope, to sustain the Church through all vicissitudes: "there you will see him, just as he told you" is a promise that where the risen Christ is, in the calm and majesty of the eschaton, there will his disciples join him.

LIBRARY
WITHDRAWN FROM STOCK
Coláiste Oideachais Mhuire Gan Smal
Luimneach

p.56